How to Not Kill Yourself

How to Not Kill Yourself

Nour Alva

Exceller Books

How to Not Kill Yourself

ISBN: 9798621356712
First published in India in 2020 by Exceller Books

Address: G1, Dream Apartment, Degree College Road,
Belgharia,
Kolkata, 700056, India

www.excellerbooks.com

Dedication

I'd like to dedicate this book to an internet user who inspired me to start writing and to the 50 people who contributed in the writing of this book because without your aid, this book wouldn't be a reality; and to the publishers, because without their help, this book would be nothing but a fleeting dream.

Most importantly, this book is dedicated to any of you who are depressed or having doubts if you are. The safest option is to get yourself professionally mentally checked if you do, even though some of you can't. Remember, it may be terrible now, but it won't stay like this for the remainder of your life. This book may never solve any of your problems, but it's nice to see that you aren't alone, isn't it?

Table of Contents

Acknowledgements

First of all, I'd like to thank the 50 senders who, for some personal reason, chose to remain under a fake name. I wouldn't have been able to make this if it wasn't for them. I am thankful for social media and I thank my friends who spread this and got more people to help. I convey my gratitude to my parents who gave me a platform to do this and last but not the least, *Allah* for giving me enough help, patience, and idea to make this.

The most frequent question I got from people is "what's the purpose of this book?" Honestly, I don't know at first. I didn't even know what I was doing at first. I was on my lowest point; I began writing everything that happened to me and my reactions to it all out. Then an internet user let me know her, just to make me know I was not alone. It lifted my spirits to some degree. Then it clicked.

I always knew I wasn't alone. It didn't feel real at first. Though I know I'm not alone, I really felt like I was, until that user came and let me know she went through something similar and that she hears me. If it can help me, why can't it help others? I don't want any more depression victims, but I knew too that I can't stop it alone.

Maybe if I start publicising other people's personal stories (with their consent of course), it'll help people who either were about to fall to depression or people who have already fallen a victim to depression, to let them see that they're not alone. Sadly I don't keep in contact with that person anymore. I don't know what happened but we lost contact, I don't even remember her at all. Thank you, whoever you are.

People with self-harm tendencies tend to think that they're alone, that no one cares for them. We do, you just need to let us. Sure, not everyone likes you, but not everyone hates you also. They need ears to listen, not mouths to lecture. Listening helps, even if you can't do anything at all.

Choose Your Friends Wisely: *Alix*

TW: Bully, Self-Harm, Suicidal Thought, Suicide Attempt

Since I was 12, I have been bullied for as long as I can remember in my school. Many horrible words were thrown at me. It's fine, I guess. I lived with those words thrown at me every day. I think I have gotten used to it.

What's worse was that I had a huge fight against my closest friend, Jean. Words were exchanged between us. Yells were thrown here and there and the nasty rumours about how I had bullied her had spread away. I didn't mean to say what I said. I wish I could undo it, but I couldn't.

This made my depression worse than ever. I had depression before, but this really made it worse. I started cutting myself again, after being so proud that I hadn't for a while. I just wanted to feel something. To make things worse, I had fallen into a very toxic group on the internet.

I don't know what I was thinking and what I was doing. All I know is that I felt bad. That's an understatement, I felt horrible. One night, I pulled out the blade I used to cut myself with. I was going to cut my wrists. I decided that this is the end. There's no point in staying alive, why should I? Everyone hates me. I hate myself.

A very close internet friend of mine, Anna, messaged me asking how life was (we greeted each other like that). I told her the truth. How bad I felt, the toxic group, the rumours, everything. Through tears, I poured out my heart through my texts delivered to Anna.

In reply, she texted the lyrics of the song we loved together. From oceans away, Anna coaxed me out of slitting my own wrists. Ever since that we've always messaged each other, despite the 8-hour difference between us. Talking to her has helped me remove myself from the group.

I stayed alive mainly because of my sisters and my niece. Such great girls needn't carry the weight of my death on their shoulders. I also stayed alive because of Anna, my friend online. What about Jean? We made peace, but we aren't as close as we used to be. Anna is my friend and I'm grateful that she helped me when I was physically alone.

Friends Save Each Other: *Volen Durcha*

What people need to understand is that you can look fine and happy to other people but underneath the mask, you're actually breaking apart and it's a huge horrible mess. That's me. I wore a mask on top of a mask and no one seemed to care about me. No one seemed to break through them, nobody even tried to.

All my life I've been through so many traumatic events and one day, I just snapped. In first grade, I met a shy little girl who quickly became my best friend, Dragon. I've learned to love her over the years and even think of her as my little sister that I never had.

I was already battling with anxiety disorder since I was 7 years old, so mental illness isn't new for me. What hit me hard was that my sister in all but blood was diagnosed with cancer. I would spare you all the details but what I can tell is that she was fading fast.

The cancer had spread all over Dragon's body and the chemotherapy she took wasn't helping at all. We both knew that Dragon was dying quick. So we lived life the fullest and I really hoped she was enjoying her last few weeks on this Earth. Like any sensible children would do in this situation, we tried to ignore her illness.

One day, we had a sleepover because we knew she was leaving soon, this would be our last chance. She grew very mad over something I said and I told her not to leave because I knew she was going to. She was too weak to go home, even though her house was only two streets away from mine.

She didn't listen to me and she ran out of the door. I was told not to run after her, and look what happened. Dragon hit her head hard and passed away from blood loss on the pavement. I couldn't take it. I couldn't believe it. What we thought was our last sleepover, turned out to be our last chance being together forever. She left me in anger. Her last thoughts of me were clouded with anger.

My thoughts consumed me and the police called me to ask what happened if I knew anything about her death. I had to tell them everything about her cancer, the fight... everything. It broke me beyond belief knowing that I was the cause of her death.

I broke down crying. I ran and locked myself in the bathroom. I don't want to see anyone else. I'm guilty and that's all I know. I took my mum's blades and I cut my own wrists. I locked the door and was positive no one would break in. I was kind of right because no one really broke in, but I was kind of wrong too because she broke into my mind.

I doubted that death was the right thing to do. I knew that she wouldn't want me to die because of her. I knew that she'd want me to be happy and have my own family one day. My family wouldn't want to bury 2 lovely children who were so close to each other.

So I did it for her. She is the ultimate reason why I stayed alive. I knew that she wouldn't want death to come and take me too. She didn't have a chance to live her life. I decided that I'll live it for her. I'll live the life she never got to live because she didn't have a choice in life but I did. I have a choice to have a spouse and have a family. I have a choice to live healthily, so I will.

Help Is Help: *Rachel*

About a year ago, I think, my classmates were awful to me. They hit me, say degrading things to me, they were horrible. I felt really hurt. It's really unfair! What have I done to deserve such horrible treatment?

One day, they decided to step it further. They told a teacher that I'd stolen money from them. I hadn't. The teacher didn't even search me even though I allowed them to if they wanted to. There's no proof that I'd stolen a hundred dollars from them.

The students told the whole school. Teachers, students, school counsellors, even the headmaster believed those liars. How could they not? Those students were seniors and I was a junior. Of course, no one would stand up to me or even believed me.

My parents even threatened to get me arrested. As I was home alone at one night, I saw this as a moment to let my depression consume me. I took a blade and slit my wrists. Why should I live if everyone saw me as a nuisance?

At that very moment, Leo, whom I knew ages ago, called me. I fell over from blood loss and accidentally hit the answer button. He asked me what happened. Leo heard me crying and sobbing, and he connected the few dots. I mean, he was smart and I'd known him for years. Leo drove up to my house and found me. He knew my parents would hurt me if I was in the hospital, so he placed band-aids on me and took me to his house.

As Leo's mum, Jenna, was a nurse, she immediately figured out what needed to be done about this situation. She helped me medically and gave me stitches so I wouldn't have such huge scars. Jenna let me stay for the night because I was afraid of going home. Leo stayed with me all night in his room and let me cry to him. I stayed away from school for a few days because Jenna told my parents that I was very ill and they believed a nurse.

When I went back, however, I learned that he had transferred to my school. Ever since he has helped me and kept me safe. I've never been alone since then until today. Only he knows what truly happened to me. I didn't get any help then, but now, I did. I still do.

I want you to do the same thing. The need doesn't have to be huge, but help's help, no matter how big it is. So whenever you are in trouble, get some help. You'll see the change.

You Are Not Alone: *Star Hearts*

TW: Suicidal Thought, Abuse

I wanted to commit suicide because I felt like I was not needed. I felt like I was not wanted, that I'm a nuisance, and I shouldn't exist. I don't think people cared anymore; no one really cared about me. People either didn't notice me or tortured me with words. It's always like that, like an endless cycle. Even my mum, every day she said that she wanted me to be dead. I was losing hope; no one really cared about me.

Never in my life have I ever attempted suicide, but sometimes, scratch that, most of the times, I really felt like doing it. Every time I held scissors or knives, I just wanted to cut myself and let the blood in me drain away, yet I couldn't do it. It's weird why I couldn't do it. I should, but yet again, I shouldn't. I don't know.

My social media account made me not to do it. I always felt alone, uncared, unwanted. As I surfed the internet, I met many people like me who were suffering from depression and suicidal thoughts, but they somehow managed to walk it off and still made artworks.

I have a lot of dreams. I want to go to Paris, I want to meet my idol, I want to go to space, and I have many, many dreams. I want to achieve those. I will not let anything get in my way.

See What Makes You Happiest & Stick to It Like Glue: *Eli*

TW: Mental Illness, Abuse, Suicidal Thought, Homophobia, Self-Harm

When I was 8 years old, I started to realise that I was 'sad' a lot. My dad left my mum for another girl at Christmas. My mum openly talked about her depression, something I regrettably made light of.

A few years later she married a man, the one who would be my stepfather. He and I got into lots of fights when my mum wasn't at home. Once I was pulled off the sofa by my neck. These arguments left me thinking that nobody would notice if I killed myself or run away.

Not even my siblings made me want to stay in that house. Don't get me wrong; those fights weren't an everyday thing. I had siblings whom I loved very dearly but they always teased me because I was the youngest. My mum is an angel when she wants to be, which is not very often.

I loved art and theatre, but they didn't really support me, which made me feel unnoticed. My voice was never heard of when my opinion was asked and I was often blamed for something I had no connections with. I honestly felt like everyone hated me.

I poured my heart out to my diary that I kept at that time. It turned out that my parents read it but decided not to get me help. My sister and my brother were getting therapy for themselves but my stepfather forbade me unless I started self-harming or attempting suicide.

My mind told me to commit suicide but I could never fully commit it. I would never let me kill myself because I loved myself too much. I would remember my friends and how much I'd miss them if I leave, so I stayed.

As I was under 16, I wasn't allowed to date, though I had eyes for a girl and a boy already. I never came out to my family except for my sister who was pretty accepting. My stepfather was homophobic. Though I never really understood why it was called homophobic because no one is scared of homosexuality; they're just mean.

There are many reasons why I stayed. I stayed because there's so much of food I wanted to try. I stayed because I never finished my shampoo and conditioner at the same time. I stayed because I wanted to get rid of my fears. I stayed because I wanted to ride a rollercoaster again. I wanted to stay because I hadn't beaten a level in a video game. I stayed because I wanted to. There are many things I want to do.

I made a promise to myself that I would never harm myself again and sail sportingly through the ups and downs of life. I haven't harmed myself for 3 years now. I still haven't gotten professional help because I chose to react this way. I know I should've. I know I should've, but I chose not to. As long as it's still not dangerous and harming myself or anyone else, I don't want to.

Don't Be Afraid to Ask For Help: *Anna*

TW: Suicide Attempt, Self-Harm, Suicidal Thought, Mental Illness

When I was 12 years old, I started to cut myself for the first time. It was because my best friend had attempted suicide. It temporarily relieved me of the numb feeling I've gotten used to. I quickly got addicted to cutting. I just couldn't stop.

When I was in 7th grade, I made a plan to kill myself. Instead of killing myself, somehow I ended up in a mental hospital. If someone asked me to describe what it feels like living there, I'd say it's terrifying. I was lonely. I didn't know anyone there, but the staffs were extremely kind and nice to me. I didn't take my medication seriously because I didn't want to be alive. No, all I wanted was to go home. I made some friends there, two of whom I am still in touch with.

I was deemed healthy enough to leave. As soon as I left, I relapsed almost immediately. My self-harm problem seemed to get worse than it was before. I let it control my life. I let it destroy myself. I stopped talking to my friends and convinced myself that they didn't care. Why wouldn't they? They did care. If only I didn't push them away... No. They didn't, right?

I either ate too much or too little, it's imbalanced. Even self-harming couldn't take away the numb feeling I've gotten since forever. Such a horrible feeling, I just wanted to feel something. I looked at the scars on my arm and realised that if I didn't stop, the cuts would get deeper and the scars would get deeper. They were already horrible to look at.

I need to stop somehow. I tried something else, anything else instead of cutting my skin apart. I tried writing and reading. I succeeded and put my blades down since January 2018, but I failed again 6 months later. I attempted suicide by swallowing pills. I felt terrible. It was a huge step back; I've stayed so long without self-harming. I felt horrible. How can I not? I just did something I survived so long without.

After that, I realised that I wanted to live after all. I was tired of feeling numb; I was tired of letting my depression control me. I'm tired of being lonely. I'm tired of losing to my mind. I decided that I would control my mind; my mind would no longer control me. I will heal. I went to another mental hospital again with the intention of getting better. I learned coping skills that could help me (and how to play cards in several ways).

I felt better and more hopeful than I did in a long time. I want to get better every day. I want you to feel better every day. I don't want to heal alone. I want us to heal together. Rise together. That's what happiness is. Happiness is contagious and I want us to be happy together. Being sad, angry, disgusted, that's all normal, but don't let it define who you are.

It Gets Better: *Kim*

TW: Suicide Attempt, Suicidal Thought

I'll be honest, I've always blamed myself. It wasn't my fault as I didn't do anything, but I always blame myself. People wanted me to change, so I started to hate myself. Why should I live if I'm a burden? I'm nothing. Someone else deserves to live my life instead.

I've tried to kill myself many times, but every time it happened, something always stopped me, like one time when I had a crush on a boy. I was 10 years old at that time. I really liked him, he was handsome and cute. Then I thought, if my so-called 'friends' didn't like me, then why should he? Why should he romantically like me if no one liked me platonically?

I'd always try to make my family proud even though I'm dyslexic. My dyslexia caused me to always have low marks. I used to be this sweet and nice girl whom everyone wanted to be friends with. If anyone had a problem, they'd always come to me, but not anymore.

I switched schools for a reason I needn't to tell. That's when it went down, I struggled to fit in because I was the new kid, and I knew no one. Exposed to new environments, I thought I couldn't do it because no kidding, it was difficult... really difficult.

I wanted to commit suicide and I wanted it to look like an accident. In all honesty, I was a coward. I'd sit in the middle of a street every day after school and every time I waited for a car to run me over, I always managed to find reasons to live, why I shouldn't die. Weirdly though, when I got back to the terrible reality at home I regretted not taking my own life.

I wish someone had told me that there's light at the end of the tunnel. I might not see it right away but eventually, I will. It's not there yet but it means I'm not there yet. I'm still fighting the battle but I'm not in the dark anymore. Others can get through it, that's all it takes, just one conversation to start it. You'll have bad days, no one can tell you otherwise, but at least you won't have to do today again.

Love Isn't As Easy As You Think:
B. Q.

TW: Suicidal Thought, Mental Illness, Involuntary Coming Out

Not that I never attempted suicide before, I can only think about it. I hate getting hurt, but I love seeing blood. I feel satisfied just by looking at it, or maybe tasting it. It's normal, right? My life wasn't exactly happy, to say the least. I was innocent. I was way too innocent for this. I wasn't even exposed to suicide, killing, or anything alike.

Things started to change when I entered middle school. I was still young, I was a shy person. I befriended people I thought I'd spend my life with, but I think I made a huge mistake. I really did. I still regret it; I still hate myself for it. I'm not forgiving myself for it.

It was only a small misunderstanding but I took it very seriously. I wrote a long paragraph about my emotions and without any hesitations or care if it'd be publicised, I sent it to Q, my friend. Back then, Q and I weren't very close. It was kind of weird when I sent it to Q. She tried to help me, it's just weird. I also told V about it. I told her not to tell anyone else, but she did. V accidentally told Z about it.

When I found out about it, I was pissed off. The friendship between Z and I started breaking off. My relationship with Z was destroyed. My only friend was Q. She still befriended me even though I lied to her. She stayed a friend and loyal to me, but I was on thin ice here.

At my house, I was also in pain as my family problems grew larger and deeper by that time. I was deeply traumatised by people shouting very loud, they triggered flashbacks of my mum and dad to resurface, and so on.

As time goes on my relationship with my family worsened and my relationship with Z slowly healed but I was still afraid. Z was a suicidal person; I was really worried about her. I wanted to help her, but I was scared... so scared! Why? I have no reasons to that.

As time goes on, my relationship with Q grew stronger, we got closer. It was hard to keep these secrets from her! It's really hard not to confess to her. I finally lost it and confessed to her. She gladly accepted it. I was... happy... but curious too... why would she accept me?

When we slowly opened up, she told me everything about herself, which was not pleasant. I can't stop crying inside whenever I remember her story. We do have our ups and downs; we're not always up like you think we are.

Weeks passed, we didn't open up to our friends except K and A. Well, we always open up to them anyway. They supported us, and I'm honestly very glad about it! I didn't always open up to my parents, as my parents are conservative Muslims and so are Q's. It's complicated.

Months have gone off and now, things just kept going down to worse between Q and me. She often hides things from me, crying a lot, being anxious, having raging anger, yeah. Q isn't really a suicidal person, but she can be if she can't control herself like this.

I'm afraid she can't control herself like this. I've been trying so hard to help her before things go out of hand, but nowadays, she is pushing me away, ignoring my questions, using harsh words. I know she doesn't mean it, but it still hurts like hell.

Dating is not as easy as it seems. Once you date someone, new feelings and new experiences occur. Feelings like you don't deserve them, over thinking, fights, and much more. Jealousy isn't something we should treat normally. No, you can't ignore jealousy. The feeling is all over us! Seeing Q with someone else, my jealousy rises. When Q is laughing with someone else, smiling at someone else, I feel jealous. It's wrong, but I can't help it. I'm trying to, though.

The worst thing you don't know is that you have doubts like, "why am I in love?" and "why is she in love with me?" It's really annoying! I don't want to feel like this but I do! I have questions on what to do, but I don't think anyone can answer. I just do what I think was right then after I'm sure I wasn't hurting her. It's complicated, but I'll try to make it not to.

Love Yourself: *E.C.*

TW: Bully, Self-Harm

Looking back into my life before, it brought tears into my eyes. A lot of thoughts flashed into me all at once. I don't think it's really that emotional or something, not that I'm insensitive, but it still hurts.

It all started when I was first transferred from my first school to my new school in 2nd grade. When I first came in, I was treated like an outsider. I mean, all new students are treated like outsiders at first, right? Anyway, that's actually another reason why I'm not good at adjusting to new things.

At my new school, my new classmates would always bully me, tease me, even shunned me from hanging out with them. That time, I was oblivious to everything so I was marked as stupid but I ignored it.

However, it became serious as later on in my life I had more schoolmates as my bullies, teasing me until I broke down. I'll spare you all the details but tears dropped out from my eyes as

I expressed my feelings in a form of rage in front of them. The rage was bad, but what's after it was worse. I was marked as a crying baby. Instead of fighting, I endured the pain alone.

When I was in 4th grade, I started drawing some stickmen and I drew anime eyes on them. I mean, all famous artists must start terrible, right? They can't draw very well at the first time, right? These kids took notice of my drawings and used it to tease me. I endured it myself, not telling anyone else about it. I stopped telling my family about these actions I've been receiving forever.

As time goes on, something changed in me. I became a copycat and copied my bullies. I just didn't want to be bullied anymore, but I realised now that I'm hurting others by doing this. I realised it months into it. I realised what I had become. People started to hate me, fear me even. I couldn't remember who I was before, but I remember I was really sorry for *who* I was becoming, *what* I was becoming.

I stopped myself from drawing more stickmen. I tried to draw chibis and anime stuff instead. It was not a good sight for my future, but I made a few friends there. We made a little group we called 'Fantasy Group'. As time went by, I was left alone as some of my good friends left away or found new friends who turned out to be my enemies later on.

School in itself was pretty much ok for me. In the morning, it's always bright; I had my best friends who were like my sisters from another mister.

As I wasn't good in my native language (which is Malay) and I'm more into English and Japanese, they made fun of me, calling me Japanese but in a bad way... I hated it. A lot of things happened, like making fun of me when I accidentally fell asleep in class, made fun of my drawings, threw stuff at me, hid my things, anything they can that's not illegal. I was losing my mind.

One day, I just lost it all. I took it out on them when my teacher wasn't looking. They backed away when I was shouting and hitting tables but I could see their victorious smirks, those very annoying smirks. I couldn't handle it and ran away from class, straight to the bathroom to cry. I washed my face, came back and back to my seat.

I snatched my broken blade from my pencil case, I was trying to cut but the blade was blunt. A teacher walked in and one of my classmates told her what happened. The teacher told them to get ready for Ashar prayer and excused me as I was trying to be calmer. She tried to comfort me. She gave me pieces of advice about my cutting tendency. I accepted her advice not to cut.

I'm still suffering from depression and anxiety. I'm scared. I was scared to admit it, and I'm still scared to admit that it's my fault. So many things are haunting my mind yet I'm still fighting against it. I still love my friends and family. I made a vow to always protect them if I can. I love them so much, I will always do. I can't love them if I don't love myself. So I did.

Everything Works Out in the End: *Naomi Tata*

TW: Mental Illness, Sexual Assault, Self-Harm, Suicidal Thought, Suicide Attempt

I suffered from depression when I was only a sophomore in junior high school. At that time, I didn't notice at all. I found out that my mother cheated and my family fought all the time. I got depressed but I kept everything I felt a secret. When I went to high school, everything's a mess. I began fighting with my mother and my father was caught cheating.

I was sexually harassed. When that happened, everyone kept their distance from me. I felt terrible. Added by the fact that both my parents were guilty of cheating, I started self-harming. I thought no one would help me. I thought nothing would help me. I felt really hopeless, despite the fact that everyone that's close to me tried to help me.

When I reached university the loads I had to carry became greater. I was rejected by multiple universities. Then I really started self-harming. I don't know why, what I was thinking deeply occupied my thoughts and hurt me, what made me think I was unworthy of anything at all.

When I really started going to campus, I experienced a great deal of depression that made me suicidal. Luckily my loyal lover helped me go through this very hard time. To think about it, I think the traumas I went through weren't that much of a great deal. Family pressures, friendship struggles, and traumas regarding sexual assault.

At that moment when I tried to commit suicide, I felt as if the world's trying to tell me something. My friends avoided me when I was harassed instead of supporting me. Instead of helping me, they asked if I was still a virgin; which really hurt me. Since then, I always feel like I'm hated, and isolated myself.

At the third semester, my family issues seemed to be better, though not the best I'd admit. I believe that everything will be better. My family issues are growing up for the better. My traumas aren't as severe as before. Stating it already means something being honest helps.

Don't Pretend You're Ok When You Aren't: *Nadia*

TW: Abuse, Substance Abuse, Self-Harm, Eating Disorder, Bully, Mental Illness, Blood

I was raised in a strict, religious, controlling family. My grandparents raised me instead of my parents. My father is a foreigner who's alcoholic and owned a bar. My mum is a singer.

Like many other baby boomers, my grandmother's super strict and controlling. She likes to check my bag, wallet, everything. She checks my body if I have tattoos, hickeys, and such. Don't get me wrong, she's really nice and nurturing. Sure, she always makes sure I'm well-fed and healthy, but she's really controlling.

I don't have any other problems than that. I mean, I've enough money, a driver, everything I could ask for. So they always say that I shouldn't be depressed, as I have everything other kids could only dream to have.

My mum registered me to an art school whilst I hated art. I wanted to be an international business student, but she didn't allow me. We have this architecture family business and she wants me to inherit it. I don't. I hated art. So at the school, I was depressed. I was required to pass a subject I had no clue on, I was required to make artworks, which I never knew how. I was expected to fulfil my family's wishes. I was the embodiment of their lost wishes.

I was bullied since I was 4 years old because I was fat, I had red hair, and I was pale... like, really pale. In other words, I was different. Not like the "I'm so gifted and I have extraordinary powers," different, but the "I'm a freak who got nowhere to be accepted," different. I also have a huge scar on my right leg, which causes the bullies to bully me more. What they don't know is that that ugly scar was the result of me almost dying and fighting for my life when I was 9 years old.

I found out that I was sorted into an art school which I was bad at. I found my style of art, which is the dark, gory style. I know it's weird, but that's what it is. As I dug deeper, I found out that I actually enjoyed darkness, death, blood, and pain. I don't know what happened to me to enjoy them.

I used to listen to dark music since I was 10 years old, but it took an impact on me when I was 16 years old when I started to turn to self-harm, alcohol binging, anorexia, and bulimia at some point in my life.

I always have been good at pretending that my life's going great. I binged on alcohol, painkillers, and I ate almost no food. I threw up the food I just ate and thought I was doing great. My only cry for help was doing something extreme, like cutting my hair to a pixie cut. That's what people like about me, my hair. Even until now.

I'm kind of better now, though I got triggered occasionally. My triggers are those bullies I've gotten before the body shaming, and the idea of having kids in the future. I recently got married but I don't want any kids. I tend to sleep a lot when I'm triggered to avoid doing things I did to myself in the past. I used to pretend I'm ok when I'm not, and that's wrong. Don't lie.

You'll Be Fine:
Salva

TW: Bully, Mental Illness, Homophobia

I'm not quite sure if this is called 'depression' already? I don't know, maybe I'm just sad and stressed? Is that depression? I don't know. I was enrolled in a local high school. My parents are really supportive of me going there. My siblings don't seem to care at all; they never really throw their attentions to me.

When I got in there, I was in total shock. First of all, public schools were LOUD. You read that? LOUD. The teachers taught as fast as light. I don't understand anything. I can't comprehend the lessons given to me. My classmates there are so different than my junior high school classmates. My new classmates there are so much more mature than my classmates in junior high school so I felt like I was seen as a snob.

I tried to stay low and unknown. Going home by public transportation, not wearing anything bedazzled, not having many friends and staying silent, all that. If there's someone who wants to talk to me, I'll just ignore because I fear I'll spew out something wrong and they'll never want to be near me anymore. I tried to study every day, even getting myself tutors even though I knew my brain couldn't handle all that stress.

I still got bad scores. It's humiliating, considering my classmates were literal geniuses. Other people expected me to be a genius too but the truth is I don't know anything. I regretted my choice of entering science class. I mean like, why? I'm not smart at anything at all. I feel like I didn't know anything, considering at junior high school I thought I wasn't this stupid.

All things considered, I began to lose hope on getting accepted in a university. It seems impossible to me, at least. If people asked me 'what college do you want to go to?' I'd always answer 'I don't know,' because I still feel like I can do nothing at all.

In the photography club, we are expected to be sociable. Well, you have to be sociable to survive here and in this world, yet I am absolute rubbish in all that. I have very few friends, I'm not bright at all in lessons, and I got more stressed as I thought 'what's the purpose of me going to school?'

That's the reason why I go home as fast as a lightning strike when the bell rings. When I look back at all my experiences past, I see that it's completely my fault. It's on me. It's my fault for not even trying to open up and let people help me.

I passed 10th grade and entered 11th. It was more stressful. I got into a new class, my photography club had a new leader, the teachers were worse in teaching us, and at first, I still shut people out so I became more and more antisocial. At that time, I almost always cried before going to bed. I was so confused. I didn't know what I'd become in the future.

I kept on comparing myself to my classmates. My classmate who sat next to me was a literal child prodigy so I got more self-conscious. There's that person who guarded the school but instead of guarding the school they found friends to have fun with and sneak them out of class to play. My 10th grade classmates liked to play with everyone except me, so I got more stressed.

I just couldn't stand it there. I didn't want to stay there anymore. I didn't want to stay in my house anymore. I ran away from my house for all the stress I faced there. I met my friend whom I'm close with. My friend looked so glamorous, and I looked like a peasant. I ran to my best friend's house.

My mother knew about my best friend so she knew where I would go. My best friend's mother was phoned by my mother because I left until 7 PM and I didn't ask for permission. I had to go home. Luckily, it was raining. No drivers wanted to pick me up whilst raining, but I was picked up by my chauffeur when my mother knew this. I told him that I needed to go to my course first, so he delivered me to my course.

After I'd finished my course, I found out that my chauffeur had left. So I called a taxi to drive me to my grandmother's house. My cousin was there too. I was asked why and advised to go home to my mother, but I didn't want to. After I was persuaded, I finally called my mother. She lectured me stuff whilst I cried.

Finally, my mum came to pick me up and brought me to a psychiatrist. They said I had anger management issues. I was told to perform therapy myself, the 4 - 7 - 8 breathing technique. To breathe in through my nose for 4 seconds, hold for 7 seconds, and exhale through my mouth for 8 seconds.

My mother started to accept the fact that I might not be mentally well at all; eventually, my father too. My youngest sibling never bothered me about it, but my older siblings sometimes did. We usually just mind our own business, though.

I'm trying to be more open, though. At first, I thought they didn't like me and they always gossip about the people who aren't as cool as them. It turns out, it's my fault for judging them negatively first. They're actually quite friendly. I started to talk with them. I played with my classmates. I have a friend whom I immediately connected with, seeing that person is just as outgoing as I am.

I'm actually more to an extroverted girl, so when I had to suffer in silence and with no friends, I was tortured because my gateway from my problems is to talk with people. I'm not the introvert type, whenever I have problems, I tell my best friend about it. When there're no friends whom I can talk about my problems to, I keep them to myself.

I actually have close friends when I was in 10th grade. Only, I was afraid to go to another class without my classmates. I didn't recognise the environment, it was so new to me and so different from what I'm used to. Their jokes are so different compared to what I'm used to. I actually have internalised homophobia. There's this femme boy in my class at 11th grade and we laughed at him together.

I was comfortable, but I still mostly hung out with my 10th grader friends. A couple of times, my friends think I like this boy. That boy became repulsed by the thought of me. I'm not sad or anything, I don't have feelings for this guy, but I also become repulsed. Like, I don't like you either. I know I'm ugly, but you don't have to get that confident or something.

If I have to advise you something, I'm going to say that everything will be ok given some time. Don't give up. Don't you dare give up in life! All of you who are troubled or who still have troubles keep on fighting. Everything will work out just fine. Eventually it will, if not now. Find people who'll bring you up, leave those who'll bring you down.

If You Can't Find a Saviour, Be a Saviour: *Nita*

TW: Abuse, Self-Harm, Suicidal Thought.

I was a victim of domestic violence. I don't want to elaborate further. At high school, I had a panic attack but no one helped me, no one brought me to a psychologist. I self-harmed. At campus, I was avoided because I'm an LGBT+ rights supporter and because of it they thought I'm gay.

I ran away from my house and didn't know where to go. It was late at night. The whole night I walked through the streets of my hometown and ended up in the town square. I wanted to spend the night in a local mosque but I didn't know what to say, why I needed a place to spend the night there. If I told them I ran away from my house, they'd definitely tell me to go back home. I didn't know what to do.

I didn't know whom to ask for help. I remembered that in the day I was aided by my internet friend Caca and I was helped to contact Yudi, he's a member of a community which I forgot what the name is. I told Yudi about my escapade, why I had run away. He advised me to stay on a friend's house for the moment and I was so confused because I wanted to ask him but I feared he'd think that I overreacted.

I tried chatting with one of my junior high school friend, Nadya, but she hadn't replied and I told Yudi that I was going home, but I couldn't. I couldn't go home. I didn't know where else I'd go. I walked for some more around the city to the square. My junior high school friend hadn't replied, maybe she's at work.

I was so confused, I didn't know where to sleep but I needed to. I couldn't just crash on a local mosque. I didn't know what to say to the mosque. The thought to just crash my motorcycle and die popped out of nowhere, but I was afraid that I'd come out with only scratches and small wounds. I saw those very high buildings and thought if I had jumped from there, would I die or go to the hospital?

Nadya finally chatted with me. She even called me a couple of times. At first, I didn't reply because I was exhausted, but Nadya kept chatting with me so I went to her house. She asked me some questions and I answered some, not all but she understood and didn't force me to answer. In the morning, I went straight home; she had some work to do too anyway.

I went to a nursing home and stayed there until the afternoon. About 3 - 4 PM. The day before, Yudi had introduced me to Karmila and she's from a local women's rights organisation. I was asked to stay at her office for some moments but I refused, choosing to go home. I've left campus, but the pressure from people around me still gets in my head.

It brings me down sometimes, but now I'm getting better with each day past. I've requested help from a psychiatrist but the psychiatrist hasn't diagnosed and I won't diagnose myself. I tried to control myself more and built a stronger wall. I promised myself that after campus, I would help people who've been through problems like mine.

Parenting Isn't As Easy As It Seems: *Linda*

TW: Suicidal Thought, Suicide Attempt, Abuse, Fatphobia

I felt I just lived a normal life in 2011. I felt that I just hold the steer to guide my own life 2 years prior, when I first had my lover (in which we're still together now). Now I'm 25 years old.

I forgot when exactly I attempted to commit suicide; I think it was at high school. The attempt was done sometime around Christmas, I think. The cause was something silly too. My mother ordered me to shower, but I didn't want to. I thought I should sweep the floors first then shower as I didn't want to make my dress dirty.

My mother thought this is a big problem. We ignored each other for 3 days. On the 3rd day, I drank a bug spray from a small container. The weird thing was, I didn't die nor brought to a hospital. I was found sleeping on a sajdah wearing a set of praying clothes. I was slapped three times to the left and to the right. I was forced to throw up and even forced to drink cooking oil to get rid of the bug spray I drank.

My parents called an Imam. The Imam gave my parents a number to contact the Imam. He told me to call him if my mum made my heart hurt again. I didn't want to. I didn't think that he could help calm Mum down. My mum said it herself that she regretted having a daughter (me) and she always kept her distance from me. I fear she has post-partum, but I didn't really care. She always seemed perfect and looked ok.

My dad seemed not to care if his house is like a hellhole or if his wife and daughter don't get along with each other. He thinks that's a natural thing. For my father, my mum's always right and I must always comply with her wishes.

Lipstick's a problem. They push me to wear a nude yet glossy one so they can be prideful with me as a daughter that's cute and pure. They force me to wear overly bright clothes. When I'm at school, I'm always scolded at. When there's a family gathering, I wasn't allowed to laugh or smile or ask any questions.

My mum would glare at me because she thought I'm ugly, ghetto, stupid, I brought shame to her name. She hates my fat body, likes to order me not to eat or sleep. She yelled at me if she ever found out that I fell asleep when I was supposed to be awake.

At junior high school, I suffered from gastritis so bad that I couldn't walk. I couldn't move. I thought I was going to die. I told my mother about it but she wouldn't bring me to a hospital, she thought I was making this thing up. Sometimes I felt so hurt that I wanted to die.

I was stressed. I wasn't sure what 'happiness' means, the definition of it and if humans ever feel 'happy'. Every day when I wake up, my heart hurts. I waited for death. I was disgruntled and miserable.

It's slowly getting better with my lover. I'm lucky that mine's caring and not demanding. I hope other parents don't make the same mistakes as mine did. They shouldn't think that children should always be devoted to them and parents need to realize that their children are also human beings too with their own likes and dislikes. Children should be appreciated as humans, not as trophies.

You Are Stronger Than You Think: *Neesa*

TW: Self-Harm, Suicidal Thought, Suicide Attempt

It all started at my high school. My parents were so overprotective. They said they allowed me to date, but they acted like they didn't want me to date. I've always been a Mummy's girl since I was little. That was until they got divorced. As the eldest child of three siblings and only girl, the burden from my father leaving us on our own felt greater on me.

I learned so hard to make both my parents proud. I got accepted to their favorite university, I always followed their wishes. The pressure was so high and it's getting bigger with each day passing. I couldn't have freedom.

The first time I cut was in high school. I play with my friends from the afternoon until early evening. Technically it's not my fault because my friend's sibling (who was delivering us) wandered around first. When I got home, I was scolded and my phone was confiscated. This thing had happened so often. They never believed me when I said I went out with my friends and not boys.

I understand why they'd be worried about me as they've been a victim of theft, at that time my mum was out of town, my dad wasn't at home as he never is, but give me a break!

Anyway, my dad read a text from one of my exes saying that I'm not a virgin anymore. It's a complicated story but it's the root to why I enjoy hurting myself because I don't have any more tears to cry and it hurts. About a month ago I was thinking about jumping off my friend's flat, I was under so much pressure, and my parents were one of them.

Now I don't live with them anymore. I go to a university in Malang now, which is pretty far from where I came from. Still, they demand many things but I can't ask for something from them. I just wanted to be noticed.

Last month I was sick and no one cared. It hurt my feelings because I always cared and loved them. Not being noticed, it's enough to bring back the depression and suicidal thoughts.

I let this sickness consume me. I smoke it off to make things worse. I placed the cigarette butt that was still burning on my hand so I harmed myself again.

In other ways too, like cutting one time, it's serious. I almost died because when I cut, I finally hit an artery. Then my lover called and I acted like everything's going fine. I'm the kind of person that can't really tell people what happened so after I calmed myself and talked to my lover.

I looked at the sky. I thought if I die now, people would grieve over me for at least a year. After that, I'd be forgotten. I want to do it just to be noticed. It hurts, being pushed aside and be number 100. At least they'll notice me but there'll be no difference. Sometimes I still had suicidal thoughts, but I resisted. I fought these demons within me.

I'll be honest (because there's no use of lying), it's not an easy fight. Some days you just want to give up, you feel your fight's not good enough. That's understandable, everyone has that. You may think no one understands, but we do. I do. I love you. Small happiness is still counted as happiness. Sadness, as little as they seem, still counts as sadness. Any progress is progress.

Never Lose Hope: *Keira*

TW: Mental Illness, Suicidal Thought, Suicide Attempt

I was diagnosed with anxiety, depression, and occasionally I had suicidal thoughts. One time I wanted to hang myself and I already prepared the rope but I was too scared. It's always like that.

My latest one was in December 2017. I just broke up with my lover and I was devastated. We are still in love with each other but we were forced to be separated. I was miserable because my lover's the reason I wanted to stay alive, the reason I ever felt happy for the first time in forever.

I checked the flat's windows and I knew if I jump from there, I'd die because I'm on the 14th floor. I prepared for everything. I would jump on our anniversary. I left a farewell video; I hoped my best friend would send it to my lover. I just wanted all this to be over with. I didn't even know if it'd be worth it or not.

My best friend found out about my plan and was disgruntled. My best friend tried to convince me otherwise. From medical arguments (it'll be physically excruciating), to spiritual arguments (your ghost will wander around), to arguments about the future (your partner won't care and laugh at you). Those were stupid arguments but I needed someone to talk to, now that I couldn't be with my lover anymore.

I felt so alone, I still wanted to take my own life. My best friend tried to chat with me every day and talked very random things so I'm not so lonely and I'd forget my plan. She succeeded, I feel depressed sometimes but I'm still fighting. She helped me fight. My problems aren't really solved yet, it's not really done. I'm still fighting, I'm still winning, my lover. Well, it's quite complicated. I still have feelings but it's complicated.

Things may not go well for us and it may not go well for you. It doesn't mean it won't. I believe that it will. You should, too. I believe my life will get better in time. I believe yours will, too. Keep on hoping.

Always Put Yourself First: *Ara*

TW: Bully, LGBT-Phobia

My mum used to be high tempered, but my dad was the exact opposite. I often have fights with my mum but I'm still the 'good' daughter in my family. I have no problems, no drama, not anything with my father like I do with my mother, but I still love her. To be put simply, we have a bittersweet relationship. It's pretty complicated.

I live in a conservative environment. I was known as an unproblematic person like my parents. I lived a 'straight' life. I surprised my parents about 2 or 3 years ago. I invited them to visit a psychiatrist. I revealed some humiliating stuff, like I failed an internship, resigned from my short college programme as my colleagues in the short college programme stressed me out, I think they verbally bullied me.

My parents think I'm traumatised, but they supported me. It just pained them to see their beloved daughter changed from an extrovert to an introvert. I hid it really well. No one truly knows how messed up I am. No one really knows the real me, a bisexual who dislikes the LGBT+ community for no absolute reason other than because the society and my parents want me to.

I kind of hate my parents, but I kind of love them too. I am an agnostic who is never really religious since I was a baby maybe. I often have fights with my conservative parents, how they're forcing their religion upon me. They never know any of what I'm feeling.

I think if people are free to believe in something, then I should be free to disbelieve. Unfortunately, not everyone thinks like that. I live in a country where it's illegal to be an atheist and I follow a religion where it's illegal to be LGBT+, and I'm agnostic close to atheist.

My parents were too overprotective over me since I was a small young child. I am a free soul. I love my freedom, I love justice. They had to ruin it. They make me feel useless, even until now.

I spend most of my time in front of a computer instead, trying to control my rage, my feelings toward my parents, especially towards my mother. I've spent my time in front of the computer from 12 PM until 12 AM. It made my mother check my high school; why I was always back so late at night. I lied to her, saying I was doing some school project.

I called my counseling guidance teacher to talk about this. The teacher was successful in making me cry. The teacher made me tell why I lied, or else the teacher would tell my mother about my lies. I admitted that I resented my mother. I wanted to escape my house. I wanted to have my own life. I wanted to achieve my dreams. I wanted my freedom to choose without my parents infiltrating them for me.

The teacher and I talked about this story, the teacher told me about how lucky I am in my life. The teacher told me that I have smart and loyal friends and that I have parents who paid for my school, and how many people out there who wished to have my life now. You may think your life's terrible, it might be terrible, and that's why you should fight for a better life. Keep fighting and it will become better with time.

Any Reason Is a Valid Reason to Stay Alive: *Tan*

TW: Abuse, Fatphobia, Sexual Assault, Self-Harm, Suicidal Thought, Suicide Attempt

I've been through many things since about 3 years ago. I'm going to tell you that I'm agnostic. I worked as a part-time teacher and I was still studying in a university. I had no one to confide to. My friends were nonexistent and my parents had problems on their own.

My family is verbally abusive. They like to comment about my weight and whatnots. That really hurt me. I never ask my family for anything, not even money. I pay my own educational fee using my own money. I'm tired. I am really confused. I want to study and work but my family wants me to help them run the shop when I get home. I am exhausted.

In my shop, there's this boy. He's a jerk; he kept cat calling me, looking at me, say things that aren't nice, like that. I told my family and all they say is "don't be overdramatic!" No supportive words!

Sure, I do love my family. I recognize their hard work to feed me and I'm sure they're tired too, but I don't like it when they become too hard on me and blame me for things I wasn't guilty of. I thought it would be nice if I just disappeared, so I began to punch myself and hit my head to the wall. I feel relaxed, like I just released the anger and frustration in me.

2016 came, I lost my job. I didn't have money, I was still studying, and I couldn't ask my parents for it. I felt so beaten and I slipped into depression deeper. I often cried, fought with my parents that I couldn't even tell because if I did, it'd be super long.

In 2017, I took a pill. I wished to overdose and die. I wondered if I could run to the car or the train, or jump to the river or may hang myself. I practised hanging myself 3 to 5 times. I searched about committing suicide. I thought about religion, about my sins if I die. Will God forgive me? What about my parents? My favourite TV series that I'll never know the ending if I die? What about my dreams and my wish to find love?

I don't want to die miserable and waste my life. I prayed to God to make me happy. My father closed the shop and tried another kind of business. I got a job at 27th of December 2017. I opened a new chapter in my life. I regret my self-loathing past. I still feel the impact it leaves as I easily get headaches.

For you who are reading this, please don't give up. You never really understand a person unless you're seeing it from his/her/their point of view. Never judge anyone. You just haven't been in their shoes.

Don't Be Afraid to Talk to Someone Close to You: *Ebi*

TW: Death, Mental Illness, Substance Abuse, Eating Disorder, Self-Harm

It all started when my mum died of breast cancer back in 2012. I was 14 years old back then. I lost my best friend and my whole world began to spiral downwards. I never really had a good relationship with my father so this made it a billion times harder. He always made problems that I must fix or cover it up because I don't want people to know that my life's a mess.

I cried every night, blaming God for taking my mother when He could take my father. I started to lose control and hate myself in 2013. I hated myself, felt useless, and had no interest to do anything. No energy to do anything, more likely.

I started drinking alcohol, smoking, and binged eating every time my father made a fuss, which was quite often. I gained a lot of weight then felt terrible afterwards and the cycle went on, I started to self-harm. I didn't want to make it clear but it went deeper up until 2016.

That time, I broke down and got into a motorcycle accident. I suddenly thought, what was I thinking? I let negativity control my life; I don't want to die now. I want to prove everyone wrong, that I'm not a mess. I want to make my mum proud in heaven.

I started to change for the better. Nothing significant but hey, any progress is progress. I started making friends, talking to my close ones, seeking professional help online and offline, limited my use of social media, limited myself from seeing my father, tried to exercise and listened to calming music. I'm not going to lie. Healing isn't easy at all. It's a difficult and long process.

I struggled to deal with my emotions and my scars turned to ugly keloids. I felt ashamed of it and I always tried to cover it up with long-sleeved clothes and stuff. After several years of trying to love myself and meditate, I felt better and made those scars as a reminder that I survived, that I'm not as weak as I think. You aren't as weak as you think. Find your strength and use it in life.

Bullying Leaves Marks: *Dea*

TW: Bully, Mental Illness, Abuse, Self-Harm, Suicidal Thought, Suicide Attempt

When I was 13 years old, I was a victim of bullying. The bullying was unbelievable, I'm not sure if they can be said bullying anymore. They called me a slut, spread terrible rumours about me. What I did wrong, to this day I never know. My parents called the school's guidance counselor. That time, they really believed what I'd gone through.

That's when my depression began. I was scared to go to school but I didn't want to stay home. My parents spoke hurtful things, just as hurtful as those rumours that were spreading out like wildfire. I escaped from my tragedies by self-harming. I thought self-harming isn't as painful as I thought it was. I ended up being addicted to self-harming.

My school guidance counselor was suspicious with the amount of time I spent there. So they called my parents again. My parents were old-fashioned. They were hard on me and thought that if I had depression, I'd become crazy. When they knew, they raged. It hurts. It really does. I just wanted it to stop. I didn't know what I did wrong to deserve their rage.

I've attempted suicide twice. Lately, I heard people saying that I shouldn't live, that I should just die, that I should stop bothering people with my presence. I stayed every day with the hope that I die. To me, life was empty and it had no meaning whatsoever. It felt like there's someone else who lived inside my head, telling me to do terrible things.

Sometimes, occasionally, I lost control over my emotions. My emotional control was terrible, maybe because I kept it bottled inside all this time and didn't confide with anyone else.

I finally gathered my courage to talk to someone, a friend of mine whose occupation is now a psychologist. The friend suggested me to meet a therapist, to get therapy. My friend got terribly saddened seeing more and more cuts in my body.

I chose to continue my education out of town, releasing myself from the current circumstances by pausing university for a year, living my life under supervision and therapy sessions. "You have to survive, for your body to stay and keep you alive."

I still haven't, I'm still not complete. My traumas are still deep, but now I'm still trying to stop hurting myself. What I can say is that bullying is really evil. It scars your heart and leaves deep trauma inside. Neither you nor I can change that, but we can choose to rise above it or to sink under it. I chose to rise. What about you? What's your choice?

You Decide the Ending of Your Story: *Novie*

TW: Sexual Assault, Substance Abuse, Suicidal Thought, Suicide Attempt

I'm a 17-year-old teen mother. I got pregnant when I was 14. The person who impregnated me left me when I was still pregnant. His excuse was that I hung out with too many boys. I told my parents and they were really shocked. My mother fainted. When things were cooler, my father came to his house, to his parents, requesting him to take responsibility. He didn't.

The first time I dated him, he sexually harassed me. He forced to kiss me and said he did it because he loved me. I left him already but he threatened to tell everyone that I dared to kiss a boy when I was still a little girl. In fear, I stayed with him. I didn't dare to fight him because his body was bigger than mine. Every time I was with him privately, he made me take off my trousers, up until I got pregnant.

When I told him, he didn't think of the solution with a clear head. Instead of talking it out, he bought bottles of alcohol and he drank it all that very moment. I was in 9th grade at that time. I was ashamed, to say the least. I had to go to school with a growing belly, I was so stressed that I wanted to commit suicide.

The 9 months I was pregnant, he didn't take responsibility. In fact, he went around busy searching for other girls. When I met him, he blamed me for having many male friends and practically told me that everything's my fault, not his. My parents called the police, but he changed the facts to make it sound like it was my fault.

Eventually, my father gave up. We let everything go. It wasn't that easy, I was terribly ashamed. I am still traumatised, that he went off with no cares in this world. He demanded that the child follows him. He thinks he has custody rights, when all the time I was pregnant he didn't help me one bit.

After I gave birth, I tried to commit suicide thrice. I realized that even if I do that, it still won't change the fact that I'm 'broken'. Nothing I do will change what happened. At that time, my grandmother calmed me. She said that strong women can do this alone, that I don't need to lose anything anymore, that God is fair, I don't need to sacrifice my life for it.

I still rose and fought for my future. She convinced me that even broken things can still be fixed. I have faith that God is fair and I can still reach my dreams. She told me how hard it seems to be, if you fight for it, you deserve it.

I changed my mind and didn't commit suicide. I'll no longer isolate myself. I'll be a better person, a better mother to my baby. I won't be swayed; I won't give everything up for a boy again. You shouldn't either. Don't make the same mistakes as I did. Don't give everything up for a boy who doesn't care about you.

Appreciate Help Around You: *Petals*

TW: Self-Harm, Involuntary Coming Out, Suicidal Thought, Suicide Attempt

My ex-boyfriend was bisexual and in the beginning of our relationship, he told me that he developed a crush on my male best friend. I was totally fine with that. I'm not going to break up with him just because of that.

Our relationship went on and I started to question if he really loved me, I started to forget my male best friend and all. I knew it'd mess up my relationship if I do ask him, but I couldn't hide this anymore. The question was burning in my head.

At June 2018, I asked him to leave me because I didn't want to do all those sweet things without him meaning it, he admitted it. He admitted that he only did the sweet things to appreciate all the sweet things I'd done for him. That he's actually interested in my male best friend, not me... not me and never me.

I acted like it was fine, but really, it wasn't. I was heartbroken, puzzled, miserable. I asked myself a million questions. Why did he do this to me? Why did he pretend that he was interested in me? I started to cut myself after a long time of not doing it. It affected my life. My physical look, my education, I was a mess. I couldn't confide with anyone because he hadn't come out yet and I wouldn't let him out.

I was so desperate. I knew what I did was wrong and selfish, but I was really desperate. I told the truth to my male best friend, my ex-boyfriend's crush. I know it's wrong, but I wasn't in my right mind. It truly relieved my head. My male best friend and I kept it a secret.

My ex-boyfriend found out I told his crush. He called me, and you can say we fought even more. I cried, he started to victimize himself. I messed up. I cut myself again. I felt more useless than ever. I felt as if there's no one to lean on, that no one loved me and that I wanted to die. I kept cutting and lost a lot of blood. I didn't get it done. I stopped. I acted like I was fine, but I wasn't.

I finally admitted that I wasn't fine and I needed help. It was hard, but I realized that my life isn't only about him. I have a future. I have friends. I have help. My friends gladly helped me, but my family doesn't know a thing. I stopped the flow of the blood with a towel, ran to the bathroom, and cleaned the blood with running water. It was a foolish thing to do because it hurts so much and the blood still won't dry off.

I came back to my room, wrapped it with tissues, hoping it'd stop. The next day, well, they had turned to dark deep scars and dry blood all over my wrist, I'm grateful that I stopped it. I stopped it by stopping the thoughts that made me do it in the first place. My family still hasn't realized. I'm glad that I asked for help. Doesn't leave much impact, but I appreciate it nonetheless.

Find a Chance to Live a Happy Life: *Love*

TW: Death, Abuse, Bully, Suicidal Thought, Suicide Attempt, Substance Abuse, Mental Illness, Self-Harm

Back in 1999, my mother died. I was 4 years old at that time. I was told that my father wasn't a good person, and sadly, they were right. No one ever told me to be strong, no one ever told me not to be sad. They told me to just pray for my mother every single day.

I was sent to live with my paternal grandmother. Things were... tough. At school, I was bullied. The teachers didn't care much and I had trouble with studying. My father would occasionally visit me and cause more troubles instead.

When I was 6 years old, I was devastated by what happened in class before, I don't need to tell it all the details but you get the general picture. Anyway, I ran outside and contemplated suicide, watching the moving cars, hoping I would get run over and I'd see my mother again.

I obviously failed the first time, but the bullying didn't stop. It continued until I was 12 years old. It wasn't just my schoolmates, but my teachers and family members too; my aunt and her new husband also abused me verbally and everyone sided with them.

My father forced me to live with him several times, but he had no proper food, lunch money, nor clothes. He would drunkenly come in the middle of the night and bang on all our doors, windows, so we let him in. He'd pull me to somewhere he wants, even though I didn't want to.

When I was 13 years old, my maternal grandmother couldn't stand to see me like this. In the end, I moved in with her, leaving my paternal family behind. Still, I wasn't safe and it wasn't really a great option. It kept me safe from my abusive father, but my maternal grandmother turned out to be verbally abusive, narcissistic and was gaslighting me... up to this very day.

I had episodes of manic depression, suicidal tendencies, and I self-harmed. I remember nights filled with crying, thinking about killing me. I just wanted to die and end all these sufferings.

Two years ago, I was blessed with 3 dogs, which helped me a lot with my mental health. They showered me with love and pure affection I never really had before. I also met my current boyfriend. He's been very understanding even though his family was really different from mine. He accepted me when I was at my lowest and encouraged me to go visit a psychologist. I'm happier than I was before. I'm really grateful for the help I get, no matter how insignificant it seems.

You will be, too. If not now, then maybe 5 years later, or 10, or 15, but it will. Just stay alive. You'll see what I'm talking about. Make some friends, even online ones count. Seek help. It's not too late to. It's never too late to.

Everyone's a Hero Inside: *G. B. D.*

TW: Abuse, Suicidal Thought, Self-Harm

My parents had different religions. My father was a Muslim whilst my mother was a Christian. Their relationship was always filled with conflict (as far as I see). They fought every day when I was a kid, but as I grew up, they fought lesser. It's not because things got better between them, but because once they fought, all hell broke loose.

My dad barely physically harmed my mom when I was at home, though. Every time I went back from staying a few days at my cousin's house, I would see my mother crying and telling me what my father did whilst showing to me the bruises. I would see the bruise on her neck and around the area of her ribcage.

Once, my father lost control when I was in my room. He looked for a knife but by some coincidence, there's none. He took cutting board and was about to hit my mother's head. He stopped when I screamed. So that's the type of environment that I grew up in, up to this day. I faced that thing for years alone. I barely opened up to my parents and I had no best friends. Who am I kidding? I don't even have friends.

School wasn't easy for me. My parents kept fighting with each other, my mother kept crying, my father was abusive (he was also verbally abusive to me, calling me stupid if I made small mistakes like forgetting today's date), I had no friends.

When I was in class, I looked out the window. The class was on the 3rd floor and I could see a railing on the edges of the wall to keep the kids from falling. On that second, the thought of jumping from that railing popped out of my head.

Will I feel the wind hitting my face as my body fall? Will it hurt when my head gets crushed? Will I die? What if it doesn't work and I stay alive? I actually thought about it for days. I planned on it, but the thought of it may not work stopping me. It'll be humiliating if it doesn't work.

When I was in 10th grade, I was still in a bad emotional state but I managed to get better that I no longer think about committing suicide. I met a friend, R. I found out that she self-harms. I noticed her scars when she didn't wear her hoodie. I asked R what that was and she told me her problems. I cried, imagining the pain she had to go through.

Weekend comes and all of a sudden I feel sad. It hurts my chest; it feels like I am suffocating. This stuff happened to me a couple of times before but this time I felt like it's too much. I took out a cutter and ran the blade through my wrist. I'll spare you the details but it felt like the pain stopped.

Since then I did that every time the pain appeared. I was afraid someone might notice. I made the scars small, except if the pain in my chest was too much. As long as I felt the pain from the cutter, the sadness and suffocating feelings were gone.

One day my seatmate, S, noticed my wrist. She asked me about it and at first, I hesitated. The way she held my hand and looked at me made me want to spill out everything, and I did. She immediately asked for my cutter (I brought it to school and yes, I did it at school as well). Obediently, I gave it to her. I never saw that cutter again.

Just that simple action made me stop any self-harming. The urge comes back once in a while, it doesn't fully stop. If it comes back, I'll either try to distract my thoughts or I'll call S and she'll help me distract my thoughts. She is my best friend of 4 years.

I wish I had known about it earlier, and now I'm going to tell you so you won't be as hopeless as I was. People care. Not everyone hates you. There are billions of people in this world, it's impossible if everyone hates your guts. Find those who don't and ignore those who do.

There's a Rainbow After a Storm: *M*

TW: Mental Illness, Self-Harm, Suicidal Thought, Suicide Attempt, Abuse

I had depression when I was in 7th grade at school. I felt as if I was nobody and I didn't deserve to love or to be loved. I like to keep my problems to myself and cry secretly, all because I was afraid of being judged. It didn't get better, actually. Unlike some others, I don't think I had it the worst or even worse for that matter. I don't know why I feel like this but I do.

When I was a 10th grader, I met a nice boy through social media. His name was E. E was the light to my dark life at that moment. We became friends, chatting here and there. Our friendship grew stronger with each passing day and finally, we started dating. I was happy, even though the happiness was temporary and it has now disappeared. I thought I healed by being with him, but it was much more complicated.

We messed up and I nearly killed myself because of him. It worsened as time went on, actually. My depression grew worse, E grew distant with me and he wouldn't talk to me anymore. My mother blamed me for everything that went wrong. The self-harming became more frequent than ever. I was destroyed and I was alone. The person I loved wasn't there for me. Negativity started to infiltrate my life.

I noticed I'd spiralled down to this mess and I intended on getting myself out. It's not easy. Thoughts of committing suicide came across my head for a few times, but whenever it came, I immediately thought about people close to me.

Please understand that pain won't last forever. It will stop. Not in a snap of a finger, but it will from time to time. It'll shrink more and more until it goes away. Be patient, life is like a rollercoaster ride. There are ups and downs, not always flat.

Nobody is worth sacrificing your life over. It may not seem like it now, but you'll see that your life is the most precious to you. That you shouldn't have it wasted on someone who doesn't care a little bit about you.

It's Ok to Have Questions: *Anita*

TW: Sexual Assault, Abortion, Abduction, Violence, Mental Illness, Suicidal Thought

When I was 21 years old, I had a boyfriend. He forced me to have sex with him by giving me alcohol. He did it again and again. He said I wasn't a virgin because when he did the virginity test, I didn't bleed. Stupidly, I stayed with him. I didn't want to do any of that, but he forced me to and I always complied. I didn't have the power in me to fight.

From time to time, I began to think that it's a normal thing until I got pregnant. Long story short he didn't want to take responsibility, his excuse was that he's still in college and he suggested me to abort. After a long argument, I decided that I wanted to abort too. I didn't want to see my parents' reactions.

The same thing happened and this time, I was pregnant again with twins. I didn't want to abort as it's my dream to have twins. On one hand, I was ecstatic; on the other hand, it was an unwanted pregnancy. I told him. He argued that the babies weren't his.

He took all my belongings and locked me in his house, forbidding me to leave. Once he punched me in the eye when he found out that I chatted with my classmate. I was kidnapped for 3 days.

At night, I rummaged through his things and found a key. I went through the fence and ran until I got to the police. I tried telling his parents but they didn't believe me, saying their son wouldn't act like that. They demanded a DNA test. I wanted a DNA test but I didn't want to marry him. I saw that he's not a good person, how good would he be as a husband and a dad?

I told my mum and my sister about it. My mum suggested that I abort whilst my sister suggested that I keep them. I was depressed and it was terrible. I didn't know what to do. Even until I gave birth to my twins, I felt like I was the most unfortunate person in the world. Whenever I remember that I feel like I want to commit suicide.

I still don't know what I was thinking by continuing my pregnancy. I know the effect will haunt me, because until now, I don't know if I've been a good mum or not. I'm trying to be, though. I made a mistake and I'm going to fix it. I don't know if I'm a good mum or not but I can tell that I'm trying to be. My twins deserve that. My twins deserve a good parent.

Seeking Help Isn't a Sign of Weakness: *Georgia*

TW: Mental Illness, Suicidal Thought

My depression was a side effect of my anxiety disorder. I was diagnosed with an anxiety disorder when I was in high school. At the beginning of it, I refused to let it affect me as I didn't think it already had. It already had. I tried to be the same as I was before, but every day it felt like there was an invisible bubble around me and it was sucking my remaining energy.

I was afraid of telling people about what was troubling me, but it was clear that it made it worse. I isolated myself further from everyone. I didn't want to let anyone in because the idea of letting people in seemed like a horrifying idea. I slept so much, I didn't eat much, I was skipping classes, and my scores were falling behind. I lost a lot of people in the midst of pushing them away.

It wasn't until months after I was diagnosed with my anxiety disorder that it was made known to me that I had depression. When the revelation dawned on me, suddenly everything made sense.

I wouldn't say I lost every single friend I had, as my high school had a lot of students, but I lost the ones that I held dearly to. I still had friends that I could say hi to in the hallways, but no one that I felt like I could rely on. Every day I would have to go to eat lunch alone and spend most of the time in class alone. My school had a big building, so walking in the hallways (although it might seem insignificant) felt horrible. It was a consistent reminder of the situation I was in.

Things became a lot worse. I admit that it was my fault for pushing people away, but I also know that I was not at fault for the pain that I was going through. Regardless, I felt incredibly guilty for the pain I'd implemented on others.

I believed that it was a point of no return, that I would never be who I was before depression. I believed that my pain was permanent and that things would never be better, that I just had to get used to the pain. It became harder and harder every day to try to convince myself so.

In a particular time in school, I realized that I didn't have anyone. Everyone in that classroom had someone to spend time with, except for me. The room had a lot of people. It felt like if I disappeared at that very room at that moment, nobody would ever notice.

The loneliness that I was going through was what led me to my suicidal tendencies. No, I never tried to commit it, but I was very close. I thought of all the ways that I could do it, I remember spending nights relentlessly looking on how to kill myself, but nothing came up.

At one point, I promised myself I would never feel as lonely as I felt. Throughout those months, I hesitated to keep going on to my therapy sessions because I wasn't sure that it's what I deserved. I didn't think I deserved it, but I realized it wasn't about me trying to reassure my anxiety. I know that I cannot live the rest of my life like I was at that period of time.

It wasn't only for me, but for those around me either. I didn't want to suffer anymore, so I needed to make sure that would happen, and I did. I removed myself from the toxic situation I was in and I had gained friends at the end of the year. I sought for help. I opened up about my problems. Although my anxiety disorder was as prevalent, I knew that things were going to get better.

What kept me alive was that I didn't question my recovery, but I just knew that I had to keep going. I kept going and going, then I realized that what I wanted really happened. I didn't feel as lonely anymore. I didn't feel this black hole in me because I filled it even without realizing it. I discovered so many things that I thought I would never discover, not even in my wildest dreams. I became happy again.

Most importantly, I realized that I didn't have to be the person I was before. I could become someone much better than her. I am glad to say I am better than who I was. There have been many points throughout this year where I thought to myself that I was so glad that I didn't commit suicide. I am glad that nothing on the internet came up that night.

No One Is Perfect: *Hannah*

TW: Death, Mental Illness, Self-Harm

I started dealing with depression when I was an 8th grader. I don't want to go to much detail but it concerns a boy (I wasn't an 8th grader yet when we met). I watched him suffer, get better and heal, only to fall back again. I blamed myself so often after that. I mean, I could've done something, right?

I didn't visit him when he was still himself, not saying goodbye. Seeing as he had a brain injury, it messed up his personality and memories. I still don't know what it was exactly and I don't intend to find out. Well, afterwards, it went downhill. He died.

That's when I started to fall, really. I just blamed myself before, but this time, it's getting real. I don't want to get into much detail about it, but the self-harm doesn't leave a physical scar. I was constantly surrounded by negativity.

I tried to deal with it by listening to some music, writing and joining fandoms. I read depressing stories but with happy endings. I tried to relate to the characters. I mean, if my favorite characters can get better, then so do I. I use writing as an outlet.

My writing often matches my current emotions. I realized that people need me. I wasn't as ignored as I thought. It wasn't much but I felt like my presence was needed for this and if I had gone, I'd have been lost.

I have a friend who's a closeted transgender and she's starting her transition. Recently, she was diagnosed with depression and anxiety. I feel like I can help her because the last time someone needed my help, I didn't. I have a girlfriend, one of my friends who needed someone to hear their rants, and my older brother. I don't want to hurt him by having me gone.

There is no such thing as a stupid reason to stay here on this planet, on this life you're living. You stayed until next Thursday because that's when your school will sell your favorite kind of biscuits? Valid reason... Find another when it's fulfilled. Your favorite band will release a new album next week? You bet it's a good and valid reason.

The World Isn't As Cruel As You Think: *J. R.*

TW: Mental Illness

The time that I found out I had depression was exactly 2 years ago. Three years ago, I moved to another country with new habits and culture. I wasn't alone since I first came here, no. I have my own family.

A year later we got a house in another city and we must move. In this new city, I felt so lonely. I was scared, I felt I was lost somewhere and I couldn't find my way home. I missed my hometown and my parents, I felt so small and alone against the world.

My husband took me to a clinic and they found out that I got depression and anxiety. I often felt like I couldn't breathe, my heart's pounding hard, and I got so dizzy. I first thought it was a heart attack. It was a panic attack. I read about panic attack way before I got diagnosed. I thought it was some kind of joke.

Now I understand how scary it is to have a panic attack. Every day I was terrified... terrified of things that I didn't even know if it's real or unreal; scared of something that I also couldn't explain; scared of being scared. Of course, I took every therapy and everything that I needed to help myself. I went to therapy regularly and never skipped a session.

Though I tried to do everything to make it better, depression made it seem different. They come and go whenever they want and they come without any warning. After one and a half years of going to therapy regularly, I thought I was already healing. Everything seemed to be nice again, I felt warm even in the coldest winter.

Then it came back again. It was in summer; the hottest summer ever in this country. Yet I felt cold inside. I felt empty. I'm denying that my depression strikes again, I denied that everything is going to crumble once again. I kept denying and then it happened. My world was crumbling down... again!

For me, the support I get from my family and my therapist is enough to motivate me to heal. I believe that this will not disrupt my future, that I will heal and be who I was before depression. I believe that I will heal if I see myself healing.

That's the thing, you can't hope for something to happen without seeing yourself making it happen. You should see you will, too. Failures and downs are expected but believe that you will rise above it all and you will.

You Matter:
Margareta

TW: Sexism, Suicidal Thought, Self-Harm

No one ever picked me first; they always made me their second choice. They're always like, "oh there's someone who's better than her." It hurts my feelings, but yeah. There's someone else who's better than me.

My parents divorced when I was little. I don't remember much about the details, but I do remember my parents visiting my father's family's house. They went through the law process and the law in the country I was always preferred mothers. They were fighting about getting my custody. My father wanted to get my custody. He carried me and slapped my mother. I immediately decided that I wanted to be with my mum.

I almost never saw him again. The last time I did, I was graduating from elementary school. I regretted inviting him. It was very humiliating. Now I don't want to invite him ever again and he never attempts to reach out to me anyway. Whenever there was a party, my friends' dads would always come. I would always come with my mum or my grandfather. I felt miserable. I felt like no one really cared. I kept thinking to myself that no one did care.

Something happened that got me to the edge. I mean, maybe the fact that I was having my period contributed it but I thought that my friends didn't care about me. I was fighting with my mum and that added to my feelings. I cried all night.

I wondered that if I die, the sun would still shine. People would grieve for a moment, but not forever. I thought about my mum. Sure, we have our fair share of fights, but I still love her. She would be alone. Who will accompany her if I'm not here?

I never attempted, but I thought about it. I used to harm myself by curling my hands up to a ball, that used to hurt a lot and those wouldn't leave scars, but little wounds shaped like a crescent moon from my really long nails. It lasts for like several days but no, it doesn't scar. I'm healing little by little. Whenever I feel the slightest discomfort, I remember my mother.

If I need to advise you something, which I probably should, is that don't you feel like no one cares. People care, just reach out. Try to reach out. Not everyone cares, but then they don't matter. Who matters are those who do. Sometimes you don't realize that some people you've been looking for all your life are really there next to you. Realize that.

People Care, You Just Need to Reach out: *Riri*

TW: Abuse, Bully, Self-Harm, Suicidal Thought, Sexual Assault

My mother is actually my father's cheating subject. So my father has 3 children from another woman and none of them knows about my existence. My mother also has 3 children on her own (before me) when she divorced her first husband. My father ended up taking care of his first family.

Rin, my eldest sister, is like my 'father'. She acts like the 'ruler'. She thinks I won't be a useful person if I'm not disciplined. Rin is also very strict, like she will get upset if I play my phone in my room. She thinks I'm a failure in this little family. Rin tells me to do this and that but she doesn't herself, like a hypocrite she is. Rin wants me to be perfect but she's actually not herself.

She always blames my mum, saying she's being a bad mum when really; she just wants to give me freedom as a teenager to play. Rin blames the way she allows me to play, once she cried so badly. Rin thinks she's the 'father', the chief of the family.

I understand that she pays for everything of mine, so she must be exhausted from work. Still, she's not my dad. In my perspective, I see my mum as my hero. I don't want her to stand up for me all the time. I want to stand up for myself once.

I struggle with befriending girls for a long time. I don't know why. From 7th grade, my friends are all boys. I know I can't continue having boys as my friends because I know people will start shipping us together and I can't let that happen.

At 9th grade, I tried to befriend girls. I succeeded but I can't ever forget my male best friend, Rafi, whom I was so close with. I still talk to him. He's the boyfriend of one of my female friends, Vina. People think I'm promiscuous for that. Rumours spread from ears to ears telling others to stay away from me. I don't know what to do. I can't keep on befriending Rafi because I don't want him and Vina to split up.

I befriended another boy, Erwin, who has a male friend, Jai. Jai was really nice. So I attempted to befriend him. I mean, if we can't be friends, ok. I still have another friend. Everyone thinks I like Jai. I don't. He stayed away from me despite everything just because he didn't want to be rumoured as my boyfriend.

I didn't have friends at all that time and that's when I started self-harming. Even though I sometimes think about suicide, I never really attempt to it... no, just self-harm. Every time it occurs, I feel numb. I'm tired of living. Every time I think of it, my friends will be like, "no, you're too precious." I think that life's too precious to throw away like that.

I just know now that not everyone's avoiding me, that I just wasn't looking at the right places. One of my new female best friends came to me, asking what my problems were. She believes that I'm not promiscuous and that I'm just his best friend.

I'm a victim of sexual harassment. My breasts were groped by a fellow student named Naufal, but I daren't to report it. Cahya, our other classmate, addressed it and I raged, like, "I never spread your problems, why do you spread mine?" After I calmed down, I tried to talk to Cahya one on one, like "what's wrong with you?"

I tried to forget it, like "everything's going to be fine." What hurts me is Naufal thought he didn't grope me and that the groping was a lie created by me. He lied so girls would avoid me, thinking I'm attention-seeking, but I wasn't. Even in my new high school, they still think like that. I grew silent. I never address that anymore. They think I'm lying but he was lying.

I was offered to visit a psychologist by my mum and my older sibling, but I didn't want to. I'm not some specimen for them to dissect. I know my family doesn't have any experience but I trust them better. I also know they meant well, but I just don't trust them.

I feel like they only want to know to get money, you know? Maybe my trust issues got in the way, but yeah. I don't know them and I don't want to spread my problems to people I barely know. I feel better now, actually. Not the utmost best, but better nonetheless. It is something, isn't it?

Don't think you're alone. You're not alone. It's impossible if everyone in this whole world hates you. There's no way fate will always be bad to you. There'll be moments when it's great and nice. Every time the feeling of malcontent fills you, the feeling of content will engulf you later

on. So keep on believing. Don't end your story.
Keep on writing it.

If You Choose to Be a Leader, Be a Responsible One: *Kaze*

TW: Bully, Suicidal Thought

When I was a junior high school student, my school created extra lessons for the 9th graders. At that time, I was so obsessed with playing games that I was too lazy to study or come to extra lessons, but what can I say? I needed it. Every time was playtime for us; I played online games with my friends. It was like that every day for 2 months.

One day when it was an extra lesson session, I saw the class's vice leader, Bowo, playing football. My friends (with mocking voices) reminded him that we had an extra lesson session and that it's not quite done yet. I wanted to remind him also, but the words that escaped my mouth were very inappropriate to say to a vice leader.

It was very rude and all my friends looked at me with panicked looks, Bowo got angry and yelled, "Who said that?" My friends sold me out. That time, I didn't know why he was angry at what I said, then I remembered that I said something that was very rude to be said to a vice leader. I apologized to him, saying that it was an accident and that I didn't mean what I said.

He didn't believe me and he didn't forgive me. He started to bully me, not physically but mentally. My mental state was really weak (as far as I see). Every day he made fun of me, insulted me, and some of his friends began to join him on bullying me.

A month went by; I was sick of it and thought about committing suicide. Stupidly, I asked my really close friend, Kai, about the best way to kill myself. Kai asked me "why would you think of that?" I poured my heart out to Kai. Kai told me that I shouldn't commit suicide because then I'd be seen as 'weak' and 'vulnerable'. Kai told me to face the problem myself and not to run away, he also told me that I hadn't fulfilled my promise to him.

I changed my mind and cancelled my plans to kill myself. I faced my problems like how a human being should. I apologized again to

Bowo (this time he genuinely accepts it) and tried to make things normal again. I learnt that everyone makes mistakes.

It's part of nature for humans to have flaws and making mistakes, but what makes you redeemable or not is if you ever try to fix it or not. If you ever realize it's wrong or not and chose to be better or not.

Believe In Yourself: Kecil

TW: Suicidal Thought, Self-Harm, Mental Illness

Well, you could say I was born into an unhappy family. My home was broken but not really broken. My father and my mother had their own different ways, like they had their own different lives even though they lived in one house. It applies to all their children. I was the youngest child. I have an older sister and an older brother.

When I was a 1st grader (approaching 2nd grade), the household began to feel more like a house instead of a home. There were some contributing factors, not just from my parents.

My parents were originally rich. We were filthy rich as we could do anything we ever want, but it didn't last long. The age difference between my siblings and I were rather far. I got to enjoy the riches for a while and not so long as my siblings were involved in a case and it ruined my family's name. Since then, I got depressed.

When I was only 8 (or 9) years old, I must experience this broken home but not really. Just because of a problem caused by my siblings, I was required to survive alone, learn how to grow up alone.

My elementary school moments weren't very peaceful. You could say I was an antagonist there. It wasn't beautiful at all, because that's when my siblings made that problem. I had to carry the dire responsibilities too. I was depressed, but I didn't know what the meaning of depression was. I didn't know that I needed help. I didn't understand what's a broken home. I didn't know that I was, well, 'ruined'.

When I was in 3rd grade (or 4th, I forgot exactly when) I was told that my sister was only my half-sister. So my mum was married before my dad and he did too. All secrets were opened. Before, I often ask my mum "why don't I ever see my dad again? Why don't we live in harmony again? Why can't we be like what we used to?"

That time, I felt utterly destroyed that I began doing things you would say inappropriate. I mean, I became a person that badly behaves as a person. You could say my physique dropped too. I was healthy, I was happy. I turned for the worst; I became an evil, selfish, weak being. I carried lots of illnesses. When I was younger, I found out that I almost died because of my illnesses.

I had suicidal thoughts at elementary school. I don't want to speak of it. I was a brilliant kid. My grades were unbelievable, but because of that condition where my family's name was ruined, my physical condition was terrible, my friendship wasn't good, I dropped and my grades dropped with me.

I was pulled out of school for a month because I couldn't take the lessons. I had to drink 8 medicines for 4 months. Until now I don't know what they're all for. Then I found out that there's a fault in my nerve system, a fault in my circulatory system.

At 8th grade, my teacher told me that I wasn't like other students. My teacher found out because my other teachers observed how often I dropped, which was unnaturally a lot. That time, you could say I was totally ruined.

My best friends left me because of my horrible actions. Everyone left. Nobody stayed. What broke me was that I really loved them. They didn't know my attempts to shield them from harm. I befriended boys. I had many best friends, none of them were girls. In fact, my female 'friends' became my enemies.

My family grew more uncontrollable, and finally, I just didn't have a family anymore. None of them were close, it's like I was alone. I'd harm myself whenever I lost control. If I didn't control myself, if my loved ones didn't help, I would not be here. I could either be in a rehabilitation center or I would be in a grave.

I suffer from depression and bipolar disorder. I've made appointments with a psychiatrist now. I haven't really healed much, but any progress is progress. I went back; I changed to be the better. I no longer force myself to work hard for anything. I can't really be bright again, fine. I have become a normal person.

My life now is better. I've never felt this good before. I realized that I had to change because I was really alone when I was little. I was young but I had to grow up mentally, I experienced moments that a child shouldn't experience yet.

I have to change. I don't care if the progress is slow. I have to be better again and that's what I'm going to get, because if I'm not getting better for myself, then for whom? If I'm not going to start with me, start with whom? Who's going to help me if not me?

Don't Be Afraid to Get the Help You Need: *Joe*

TW: Self-Harm, Mental Illness, Sexual Assault, Suicide Attempt

I'm not really close with my parents or anything even though they're family. It feels like 5 strangers are forced to live together in a house. My father is quite distant and so is my mother. Most of our interactions are nothing meaningful. My siblings aren't that bad. I'm very close to my second brother. I'm the youngest sister. I am not as close with my first brother as I am with my second.

I am a college student. My father is currently sick and I have mixed feelings for him. I was emotionally attached to my boyfriend. One night I had an anxiety breakdown and he wasn't available to help me go through it. I had to take care of my father whilst studying for a midterm test. That night, I cried so hard that I couldn't control myself for maybe half an hour to an hour.

After I cried, I felt calmer. I don't know why, but I had cut myself. That somehow calmed me.

The next morning, I visited a psychologist. She told me to visit a psychiatrist instead. I've been doing psychotherapy and taking meds. I realized that I went too far. Something had to be done. My psychiatrist told me that I'd been holding too many secrets on my own, that I needed to open up. I don't really trust people. I don't think anyone would care enough to help.

I was also a sexual harassment survivor. I don't want to get into much detail about it, but it was by a stranger and I was a 2nd grader. I attempted suicide once and harmed myself twice. I felt so hopeless, like I couldn't do this anymore. I've had enough.

Before the incident, my college mates were deafening in the group chat. Somehow it got into my nerves. I left the group, turned my phone off, and harmed myself again. I just can't stand loud sounds. My father yells a lot. I mean he's sick so he can't really control it, but yeah. If I hear any noise, I immediately have an anxiety attack.

That night, I was at my lowest. I hate the fact that I'm emotionally dependent on my boyfriend and that he wasn't there to help me. I just fear I might do something dangerous if that happens again.

Our relationship was troublesome. His parents didn't approve of us dating as we have different religions, but I still love him. I tried to let him go for so many times, but I always fell back to his arms. We knew our love was only temporary, that we wouldn't bring it to the next step, but we're still hanging out. His mum always asked if we're still calling each other at night, which we used to do. I couldn't sleep if I hadn't called him.

My friendship is pretty much usual. I don't tell my problems whatsoever to them, until the incident. No, I usually talk about other things. After the incident, I began to open up to my closest ones. Even then, I didn't tell them everything.

My psychiatrist prescribed me meds for my bipolar disorder, anxiety, and depression. There is nothing wrong with getting help. This is my way to be healthier. Going to a psychologist/psychiatrist isn't a bad thing.

Listen to Your Children: *Brooke*

TW: Abuse, Incest, Self-Harm, Mental Illness, Bully

My relatives were toxic, to say the least. My parents were emotionless and it was always hard to talk to them about anything. Well, my father was the hardest. I cannot recall any happy memories with him.

My two brothers sexually abused me. It started when I was a toddler and it was casual. I don't want to go into much detail about it, but it changed from 2 of my brothers to 3. I have 4 older brothers but only 1 was kind of nice to me. Anyway, all my brothers moved out already.

I cut often and a few times they were seen were by my mother and oldest brother. My oldest brother laughed and shrugged it off. My mother scolded me, saying I was stupid for doing it.

I'm a high school student. Let's say my high school things are not great due to my social anxiety and deprivation of socializing ability. I have a best friend of 8 years, Lindsay, and neither of us have other friends because we never really socialize with new people.

I've never been bullied, but there are a couple of people who hate my guts and tell me that they'll be happier if I'm dead, but that's about it. Well, my house was more destructive than my school. I cry more at my house than at school.

Lindsay and I used to hate each other because I was popular and obnoxious. Then one of my close female friends, Julie, started talking to her. Eventually, the 3 of us warmed up to each other. Sadly, I didn't keep in contact with Julie. We actually ended the friendship in either 3rd grade or 4th, I don't exactly remember. Like I said, we were exclusive.

I did have difficulties in school. Most of my teachers disliked me because of my loud personality, including my headmaster. I got in trouble every day and I was sent to the headmaster's office. When I was in junior high, I think, I had anxiety. I rarely ever got into trouble because I just went with the flow and kept my mouth shut. (how to keep your mouth shut when you're loud? You get it, right?)

In 7th or 8th grade, my English teacher sent me to the office almost every day. My brother would give me rides to school and he always made me late. The headmaster hates me, or at least I think he does as he always glares whenever I walk by. Now my teachers like me except for the ones in the office, like the secretary.

I don't have a physical abnormality, but I most likely have a chemical imbalance in my head. That would explain my behavior, but as I say, I can't really get it checked. My relatives wouldn't hear me, after all. Now I'm just trying to live my life the best I can, ignore what they say and care about me. It doesn't mean I don't care about others, I learnt that I better care about myself first.

In Bad Times, Try to Find Some Good: *Stella*

TW: Death, Suicidal Thought, Self-Harm, Suicide, Mental Illness, Abuse

My home life was ok, but not my friends'. My friend (A) came to school crying every day. My other friend (B) and I tried to console her, and eventually, A told us that she's suicidal. We were shocked but we tried to be supportive. B didn't come to school for a week because her father died of cancer. A then came to school with cuts on her arm. She almost did what I feared.

I was a 6th grader. I told an adult because I didn't want her to kill herself. She was angry (which is understandable). She said some horrible things to me. Another friend of mine had cancer (which B's father died of) and my other friend Malik just committed suicide. I didn't stop him, even though I know I could've.

At that time, I feel like a horrible person. Depression is horrible and not a joke. It nearly took A and B, and it took Malik. All this started to take me away. I honestly questioned my worth. Was I a terrible friend? Why was I a terrible friend?

Another friend of mine (C) would come with scars on her face and red marks all over. Her father did it. He hits her. Yet whenever she speaks about it, he always finds a way to blame their cats. Not even her brother would help her. Her father almost severely injured her and she finally ran away. She lived on the streets. She was slowly dying. She told my other friends and me where she lived, and now she started to live with her other friend. She's happier now.

My new school is better now. I haven't been attracted to anyone yet, I think I'm aromantic? I'm still questioning my sexuality; I'm not in a hurry to know it. I have years. My new school is definitely better.

I've never attempted suicide, but like I told you, people around me have. No, I've never really harmed myself. I learned in 6th grade to never do things to myself, but I still question my worth. Am I really that bad of a friend? Maybe it's just that I have a guilty conscience, if I call someone a jerk, I'll spend the next few minutes thinking I'm the worst person in the world.

I had a panic attack once, when one of my friends was about to commit suicide. I started sobbing, shaking, I lost control of my breathing, and I was nauseous and lightheaded. Nobody really saw because I ran to the toilet. A friend of mine, Zoe, arrived and started to talk to me in a soothing way. She made me practise mindfulness. She took me to the guidance counsellor.

I still thank her for those helps. I may not have healed completely, I may still have those traumas, but I think I'm making a progress, and that's fine. Whenever I have a panic attack, I remember to calm down. I remember to stabilize my breathing. I remember to breathe correctly. I remember to try to clear my head. I remember I'm still alive and I should continue it.

Everyone Has a Dark Side & a Light Side in Them: *Anemone*

TW: *Abuse, Suicide Attempt, Suicidal Thought, Bully*

My life wasn't all about what's called toxic, but the toxicity made me die slowly. There was always a fight in my house. Ever since I could remember, my parents always argued with each other. My neighbors always talked behind our backs, yes we knew, because who wouldn't?

As I was raised in such high intonation from both sides, I became a temperamental person. I still go to school. I easily got pissed off over small matters; Mother versus Father, Mother versus me, Father versus me. All three of us had our own ego.

I remember the foolishness that came with my ego. When I was 4 or 5, I told my Mother that I would kill myself if I didn't get what I want. She told me "go ahead." I ran to the side of my house in which it was under construction. I climbed on a wall of bricks. I looked down. I hesitated to jump from 1 meter. It was stupid but somehow I still remember it until today.

I'm forgetful. Sometimes I can't remember what I did or said yesterday, or even a few hours ago. I only remember a few things that leave trace. I liked to be alone sometimes. I just sit on my desk during break, playing with my phone. Sometimes I go to the cafeteria alone then to the class, sit, and phone again.

I attempted suicide several times. I forgot since when, actually. I think about "how to die in the most painless way?" maybe when I was 15 or maybe younger.

I had friends, but not close. I couldn't keep a relationship with people. In high school, I envied my friends who were always together wherever they went. They even slept over in other's house, having pyjama parties, talking about boys and fashions during weekends. They were going along so well.

I only had two most visited places, home and school. Oops, sorry, I meant *house* and school. It was not a home; for me, at least. It was merely "my parents' shelter where I had to spend a few years of my life in."

I didn't go to prom in which it was almost every girl's dream in their teenage life. I remember I was going out with Mother in the evening for groceries. We were driving across my high school. I could see the shining light and the music in the yard. Yet I couldn't come. I was bullied in high school. Some people looked at me with disgust. I knew I wasn't pretty, sexy, and funny. I was a cloudy cloud.

I used to like writing. In elementary school, I wrote a "spooky" story in my notebook and my friends liked it. I forgot why I stopped writing at that time until I tried to write some random short stories in high school. I posted it on my social media page and shared it. Some said it was good and some said it was bad. I was okay with that.

I made a huge mistake that I regretted to this day. I showed them to my Mother. I asked her to read them and gave her opinions about them. She said "they are terrible," with no glance at all. She didn't even look at my computer screen when I was asking. I kept thinking about it and I was never able to finish any of the stories I made.

I kept making a new one with a new idea but it never came to an end because it was terrible.

Oh, and I used to like drawing. Father liked to draw things in his way. I wanted to be able to draw what's inside my head. I liked anime and manga at that time, so I wanted to draw my favorite characters. I couldn't really copy the figure inside my head on a piece of paper. I tried as hard as I could. I wonder why I didn't ask my Father to teach me.

He saw me drawing one day and he said, "You keep drawing the same thing. Are you dumb?" Yes, Father, I am. I didn't know that it was that hard trying to make you proud of me. Again, I stopped. How to die in the most painless way? Is it overdose? Is it by drinking poison? I had a dream to die in my sleep.

I began to have *my* life after I enrolled in a university, which was out of town. After 3 months of living with my aunt I separated from my *family*, I felt so much better than before. I had friends from my first class. We exchanged numbers, took some selfies, visited their boarding houses (most of them were from different cities), and did some stupid things together.

I realized *it* was because of the high tense pressure created in the family. The thoughts of ending my life were from the toxicity created in that house. I began to be able to control my anger.

My relationship with Mother got better. We often spent time together and often shared laughs together. We still had fights but it didn't really hurt me much, maybe because I was already immune at that time.

You know, after the things that happened before, I learnt many things. I didn't recall myself thinking about ending my life. I just wanted to spend my days with what I really like to do without anyone forbidding me.

Father and I almost never spoke. Even when I went *home*, we never said a word. Every talk we tried to make always led to an argument. He attacked me once. It wasn't the first time he hit me but I could see the hatred in his eyes. I was terrified. I screamed and called Mother. Again, we fought; Mother and I versus Father. At this time, I clearly knew what kind of person he actually was. Everything came from him. The problem was him. He made us like this.

Soon, I knew that Mother loves me in her way. I believe that she loves me. She loves me with her best. She fights for me. She went through terrible kinds of stuff for me, or even worse.

I'm not trying to make Father look bad because he is still my Father no matter what. I never know about his thought on me. I like to collect people's opinions on me, but not his. I never asked him until his last breath. Was it my mistake? I don't know.

I was afraid to hear bad things from him and triggered me to be the old me. I only had a small circle of friends in real life. I had some online friends since I spent most time on my phone. I can't really mingle with people in real life. Well, maybe because I wasn't pretty, sexy, funny, and popular.

On the other hand, I gained a strong relationship with people online. I was free to say things I couldn't say in real life, besides cursing. Friends make me feel like I'm not alone. Though some left, but that's life. I thank every one of them, including those bullies I had in high school.

I no longer care about what you say. I'm not usually open to talk about my personal life and my family. We went through a lot of things and they can't be solved so easily. I can't be someone that people expect me to be. Those memories are still tingling inside my head. The thoughts make me worthless when I actually can fight them.

Now, it's me versus me. I'm a 23-year-old girl who is still afraid to face her days, to be honest. I'm afraid that one day I'll be a failure. I'm afraid that I'm really worthless. I'm afraid that one day I can't do things on my own. I fear that one day I'll disappoint Mother. She is everything to me. I don't want to make her sad anymore. I don't want to see her in tears. I stayed alive because of her. My parents and my friends are everything to me.

If one reason can't keep me up, then I will look for another... over and over. I will dig the ground even if I have to. I must. Even though no one will know what will happen in the future, I will try my best.

Nobody is perfect, no one will be, but why don't you give it a try? It's not a regrettable thing; it shouldn't be a regrettable thing. As long as you're not hurting anyone else and yourself, why don't you give it a go? It might be useless, but it also might be not and you'll be grateful for what you do. What might scare you is the anticipation, but trust me, it'll be fine.

It Won't Last Forever: *Robin*

You could say my home life wasn't so great. My mother was ignoring me and my stepfather was always drunk. He'd always play some loud music and I couldn't focus. He'd throw up in the sink and I had to clean it up in the morning. Now, I can't wash the dishes without wanting to peel my skin off because I think of him all the time. It's frightening, what he'd become. He always yelled at me for being fat and accused me of sleeping with someone even though I was just 12 years old.

At one point he was so drunk that he slapped my butt, I shoved him away. He played a big role in my depression. The things he said made me feel like I was nothing; he treated me like a huge stress ball that he can scream at.

Whenever I needed help with homework he'd say I never tried and that I was an idiot. I couldn't even ask the teachers for help. I started failing school. It's worse because it made me feel stupid. Everyone told me that I was overweight and that I should go on a diet, but really, I wasn't feeling much. All I did was lie in bed or go to school. I'm just so tired of everything.

At school, people talk about me of being fat, dressing weird, and basically creepy. I actually believed them after a while. At some point, some kid took my headphones on the bus, which was upsetting because everything was so loud and I couldn't handle that. I panicked and hit him. I couldn't stop. I had to get off the bus.

I sat in a bush in my porch and hid, I felt really bad. It was weird. I tried to strangle myself and stabbed my arms with branches but it obviously didn't work. My mother found me and we talked about it. We spoke to the headmaster at my school about what happened. He said it doesn't matter because that happens all the time. It made me feel like my panic attack didn't matter, like I didn't matter at all.

I started looking at ways to hurt myself or to kill myself as I didn't see a point of living. I started cutting and my mother saw, she said she'd beat me to death if I ever do that again. Fast forward to about 3 years later (9th grade), I started cutting again and I was planning to kill myself. I was completely ready even though I had friends who loved me and told me they'd miss me when I die.

Then I had a doctor's appointment and I had to fill out a form. I decided to tell the hospital what I was feeling, how I completely planned to kill myself. They spoke to me for a few hours. They decided to let me go home and set up a plan to help me.

I had to give it to my most trusted family members/friends with all the things that could trigger me. My mother freaked out when she saw 'washing the dishes' was in there. I felt pathetic having to follow this plan but after a while, I started feeling better and less hopeless. I realized that I'd survive this, even if it's hard. My life wasn't over as I made so many mistakes and I wasn't perfect.

Through all this, I was failing school, constantly dealing with health issues, dealing with a very severe mental illness, and coming out as a trans boy to my very transphobic family.

I also had thyroid failure and I couldn't digest food without taking pills, which was a huge problem because everything just felt so difficult when my body hurt because of those issues. I didn't want to keep dealing with the pain it always caused and the stress it put on my family. I couldn't go to school because I always went to a hospital so I wasn't there most of the times and failed most lessons. I felt dumb, like I'd never succeed.

I'm diagnosed as schizophrenic; I wasn't on medication for it yet. My mother sent me to therapy but took me out because I mentioned her. She didn't want to know that she's part of the problem.

I finally decided to come out as a trans boy to my mother's side of my family, even though they're really homophobic and transphobic. She was very upset. She still hasn't come to terms, but she is trying more. She said if I tell anyone else about this, I'd be kicked out, and I may not get a binder or anything. I was constantly dysphoric and felt she hated me for it. I'd never be able to be myself, so what's the point of trying?

Then I went to the hospital again, I had to go to therapy again or I had to stay in the hospital or move in with my father. She doesn't like me but if I move in with my father, she won't get child support or something. I don't like her either but my dogs live here and at one point I didn't try to kill myself because I knew, if nobody loved me, well my dogs did and I can't leave them like that.

On the contrary, my father is really sweet and supportive of me. He's the exact opposite of my mother. He's also been depressed before he met my stepmother. I was constantly worried he'd commit suicide. He knows about my mother and me, actually. He and I are close. Very close.

He doesn't know about my gender identity, though. I've always been scared of his reaction even though I know he's supportive of all that stuff, the fear's still there. It's still there. He tries his best to raise me even though he didn't have parents when he grew up, he didn't know how to act as a parent. He's an amazing father, I love him so much.

When I was in kindergarten, he lost his right eye and still affected by it a lot, but he's still funny, sweet, and caring. He tries his best to make me happy and have fun, even though he's upset.

I have a friend I can come to talk about this. Her name is Amber; I met her at the beginning of 9th grade in gym class. We just casually talked and then we started hanging out at lunch and before school.

After a while, she stayed a night at my house. We talked about deep things and then after a while, I told her everything that'd been going on with my life. When I started cutting again, she was there. She told me that she understood what happened. No one had ever been there for me before so it felt weird.

I mean, my other friends all listened to my problems but they didn't try to help or give me advice. She's the only friend I have that I can trust like that. The one whom I can really cry to and she won't get upset.

Last year, I was in a relationship with someone for 6 months. It was a long-distance relationship. He always ignored me and stuff, he only texted me once in a few weeks. He overdosed and went to the ER. He had all his family to tell me that he was dead so he could see how fast I moved on. He came back once I was going to move on, calling me a 'cheater'.

I still got together with him because I didn't know what it's like to live without him. He made me push away my friends and he cheated on me a lot. When he disappeared for too long, I'd get upset and he'd tell me he got in an accident or he got sick, but it was all a lie. Then he broke up with me last Christmas. I realized I didn't need him as much as I thought I did.

I stopped harming myself a bit ago; the suicidal thoughts have gone way less than before. I'm not exactly sure what made me stay in this world. I went to therapy and she said it'd be ok and she'd help me. I realized I was not completely a lost cause.

A bit of a reason why I wanted to kill myself, well, I already failed high school. I thought I wouldn't get a second chance in life now, but then I spoke with my mother and she told me how she didn't go to college and her life isn't so bad. She made me realize that I could survive without being perfect, going to a prestigious university, and doing something extraordinary. I can be ok and be happy being small and have a nice job.

Also now I have a boyfriend that I've been with since 12th of February, he's also from far away but he's going to visit soon. His family doesn't really like me, though. He's one of the reasons why I stayed. There are numerous reasons why I stayed.

Though there are reasons to kill yourself, there are reasons to stay alive. Find it, find them. Embed them in your brain.

Not Everything Must Be Solved Overnight: *Winter*

TW: Homophobia, Abuse, Self-Harm, Suicidal Thought, Suicide Attempt, Bully

My mother doesn't know anything because of my stepfather. My stepfather is the reason why I won't come out, as he's a man of the Bible and is always looking for any excuse to kick me out of the house. They both constantly make fun of gay people and use the word 'gay' to describe something horrible. He said that gay people don't deserve to get married and that made me hide who I am.

My house is filled with four of my half-siblings who are treated way better than I am by my stepfather. I'm always the one getting into trouble for no reason at all and got punished for nothing. He never liked me and liked to pick fights for nothing. My mother knows about this but won't defend me or anything as she thinks I deserve it. She only hears his side of the story.

My father lives 3 hours away. His house is the only place so far where I've actually been happy. He knows about my sexuality and willingly attends a pride parade with me. He's the complete opposite of my mother and stepfather.

My friends told me I should just move in with him, but then I'd lose everything I had here, and as stupid as it sounds, I don't want to. My friends, my life, basically I'll be a new page and I don't want to lose that much. I see my friends hanging out but I can't. It's the price to pay, I guess.

I have 4 stepsiblings. The 3 of them are still really young so I don't consider their behavior as anything as they're still children. The other one is in her pre-teens. She's not the nicest sometimes as she'll take her father's side to anything and gets me in trouble. She may be a devil but she has seen me harm myself and slowly tried to make me stop. She always does small things that do help me out in the long run.

I don't feel accepted much and I feel like I don't belong in some places. That feeling is what subjects me to loneliness and the feeling that no one actually cared about me. I've had this feeling for a while now. I've tried to kick this feeling out of me but I'm always sucked back into it.

When I'm enjoying myself, it goes away but I always know it's just tucked away in the back of my mind, waiting to haunt my days again with suicidal thoughts and such thoughts even made me attempt it. I don't know where it goes most of the times.

I'm a high school student. My elementary friends all went to the same high school where I went. I'd lost some friends as I wasn't 'popular enough', not for my old ones and not for my new ones either.

My other elementary school friends are kind of like me. I don't need to specify all that but we tried to help each other whenever the other had a bad day or something, but I still have doubts whether they actually like my presence around or they're just being kind.

The school itself was ok I guess. It's like your normal typical high school but hopefully, I wasn't talked about or just good things. No one seemed to care about the rumours spread about me when I was a 9th grader. I wouldn't say what the rumour was but it really hurt me. My ex-friend who spread it saw it's the only way to save her reputation. Still, I'm grateful that at least people now are either forgetting it or ignoring it.

My teachers are kind of good for me, but I realized that they never really cared about their students, so that's that. I mean, there are a couple of teachers that I can talk to but others won't even care about the problems that their students face.

I also had broken up with my girlfriend as she went to a different high school and she didn't want to continue our affair as people would give us disapproving looks. I think she was ashamed of me. We remained friends nonetheless. I've moved on. The relationship was nice but I don't need that self-doubt when I'm already dealing with lots of it right now.

After getting out of that relationship, I realized I'm better off alone to take time to actually heal. I don't think I have completely healed yet, but I know I'm going to, and I really appreciate myself trying. I know this isn't an overnight thing at all, and some fails are expected, but I'll heal. I'll reach what I've lost. I'm going to. I must do it, for me.

Your God Is Always There By Your Side: *God's Army*

TW: Mental Illness, Bully, Sexism, Death, Suicidal Thought

Depression is something bad in our lives. I felt that when I was an 11th grader, I think. I've been a victim of bullying for a long time, from elementary school up to tenth grade in high school, actually. Maybe it's because I don't adopt toxic masculinity and that I act sort of feminine. My character's just soft and I've been called many rude things because my character doesn't usually go along with 'boy'. I don't know if that's really a good enough reason to feel hurt, but I am hurt.

My mother passed away. I loved her dearly and I practically idolized her. I lost the very person I loved more than myself. She had ovarian cancer. She survived it for a while but not long enough to kick it away. My sister and I have

142

accompanied her to go get medications and such for more than a year.

I understood well enough how hard it must've felt, how much worse the pain must've been for the sufferer. It pains the bystander to watch it; the sufferer must be in greater pain. Every night I compressed her coccyx with warm water, especially after her chemotherapies. The effects of the medication affected my mother's coccyx, and the effect wasn't a pretty sight.

I used to think that maybe she could transfer some of her pain to me so she wouldn't have to do this alone. She scolded me and said that I mustn't think like that, that her pain was only temporary, that Jesus was testing her and making her a better person than she already was. At that moment, my heart was touched and I was convinced that she'd heal.

Jesus intended something else and He took her to reside in His home in heaven. After all that, I began to feel depressed. I practically lost my mind and soul. I don't know why, but I began to be obsessed with dark music, my mind kept telling me to go chase after Mum. I began to suffer from anxiety, and it's quite disturbing. Scratch that, it is really disturbing. It goes unnoticed, none of my family members except for maybe my sister realized.

I was baptised by my church. I was baptised when I was in 12th grade, after my depressive moments. I realized that all this time I was lost and misguided. The revelation made my heart break. I was crying heavily. I repented and begged God to raise all my troubles in my life. It really happened. It really happened! God healed me and fixed my life even though I disappointed Him. He forgave all my sins and loved me. He's real and I feel that.

Never lose faith. Even if you don't believe in a God, believe that you have the strength to keep on. Help will come in various unexpected ways and forms. Help always arrives and don't be desperate.

You Can't Do This Alone: *Tyler*

TW: Mental Illness, Abuse, Bully, Self-Harm, Suicidal Thought, Suicide Attempt

I've had severe depression, suicidal thoughts, and other things since about 5th grade. It was mainly caused by trauma, abuse, neglect, and other things.

My mother was a little bit weird and did a lot of things she shouldn't. I was enchanted under her spell. I was completely unaware that it wasn't a good environment for me to live in as a child. She isolated me in her house. I didn't develop the right social and emotional skills because she almost never let me out of the house, pretty much didn't let me properly grow like all others.

Some legal things happened after she illegally moved me across state lines and now I live with my father and my stepmother. That happened halfway through 4th grade.

I struggled with basic lessons. It was my first time in a public school. I was bullied in both languages. The bilingual kids didn't know I already knew Spanish because that's the only thing my mother taught me very well back when I was younger. 4th grade kind of borders some of my memories. Those are what I struggle with now; the bullying, abuse, and forced-rapid social growth.

I wasn't really able to hold on, as there was pretty much nothing to hold on to. I didn't know what 'depression' actually means until I was in 7th grade. I just knew that sometimes I'd start crying without me knowing why. It was a challenge for me to find motivation to move, to breathe, to think, to do basic things. I'm just so tired of it all.

I've worked on how to be better, little by little, week by week, and sometimes I still got worse all over again. It's so hard not to. I was doing well at 5th grade but somehow I crashed back down at 6th grade. I was doing well again at 7th grade, but I wanted to die at 8th. I hadn't struggled that much before, but now it's happening all the time.

I have attempted suicide many times before that I couldn't possibly count them all. As I didn't know what I was really doing, it didn't work. I didn't want anyone else to know, so I struggled with it alone. That was my mistake, really. I shouldn't have gone through this alone, neither should anyone.

I had court-mandated therapy as part of my parents' divorce. It didn't do anything. The therapist was more interested in making money than she was in helping me, so she never really helped. I moved to another state, and after years of struggling alone and hear others talk about their therapist, I asked to see one.

I found one who's absolutely amazing. I mean, I've only been with her for a year but she helped me through so much trouble I'm going through. I'm very glad I am appointed to a useful therapist. Therapists are an important part of a support system, but so are friends.

You need people who can be with you on your bad days, on the worst days, and help you through. Hitting lows doesn't negate your process. It's part of the process. The lows you hit, they'll get shorter and farther apart. It's ok.

Mistakes Are Part of Life: *Nraqell*

TW: Suicidal Thought, Suicide Attempt

I'm an only child. I used to wish I had a younger sibling. I am what you'd say a good child, but after years past, after meeting new people with all kinds of thoughts, I slowly changed. I became lazier, tired more often, things quickly annoyed me, irritating and pretty much like an attention seeker, but I wasn't really seeking one. I lost a lot of my family and my friends in time.

I once had tried to commit suicide because I thought I wasn't a good child to my parents. I often cried alone, I never really showed my pain to others. I never really showed that I was in pain and I didn't really seek help.

Two years ago, I met 3 of my friends. They came to me for a message from me. I'm really happy I helped them; they were so desperate back then. I helped them then, I saw they were healing well. I noticed that I was next in terms of being desperate as I didn't tell anyone my problems or my pain. I wanted it to stay like that.

I thought I wanted it like that. I stopped for some time, but sometimes I kept going. It's complicated to explain.

I'm positive enough to change my mind about killing myself so I've not worried my loved ones. I mean, I lost my father when I was very small. He left my mother and me, but I still miss him. For some reason, I still do. I stopped because my mother is too precious to me. I don't want to hurt her or make her cry, I love her too much to let that happen. My friends helped me and I'm very thankful.

I would advise others to just be yourself, don't neglect your family or friends, love yourself, and never let anyone else define who you are. You know the best of your own life condition. You know yourself more than anyone else in this world. Your family and friends love you more than you'll ever know.

Find People Who You Can Trust & Tell Them What's Happening: *Krissy*

TW: Abuse, Mental Illness

I have both my parents alive, but it feels like I only have one. My dad isn't really in the picture even though I meet him every day. He doesn't really talk to me or my sister and he's verbally abusive to my mum. My mum has always been loving, but lately she seemed to be aggravated at me.

I'm closest to my younger sister, Carly. I also have 2 half-brothers and 3 half-sisters from my father's side. They're all at least 20 years older than me. I never really talk to them and I don't particularly like them. I have a half-brother from my mother's side that's older than me by 11 years. I wouldn't say I'm extremely close with him but he's a good older brother and I enjoyed his presence.

I'm an introvert and a very shy person when I meet people in real life. It may not seem like it on the internet, but in real life, it is. I don't speak up a lot so I only have very few friends.

I'm still in school right now. I take college extra classes and high school classes. I'm an A student and I've always been. I'm a big-time procrastinator, though, and always have been. That causes me a lot of stress. I have a good memory so I rely on that a lot more than learning the material.

I've had one real job in my life at a nursing home, helping with activities, serving foods and drink. It was last summer this year. The nursing home was fantastic. The people there were awesome. Though I always found myself second-guessing myself and would often think of myself as trouble if I don't do exactly as they say the first time.

I was and am terrible at talking to people. Keeping a conversation up with people, I would try my best to, but it feels like it wasn't enough. I have a small circle of friends that I feel comfortable with even in the silence, as I have mentioned before. I also have a circle whom I consider my 'friends' but aren't necessarily comfortable with them if it's just them and I.

I think I have a lot of people who do care about me or are kind to me but I only talk to one or two on a daily basis. That's my mistake and I admit. I have too deep of a trust issue and I have to change it.

I've most of my friends for more than 6 years. We are more than willing to enlarge it, though. Most (if not all) of my friends must reach out to me because I am too scared to. I tend to keep my distance until they have made it clear they want to and intend on being my friend.

Half of them were my classmates, whilst the other half were my neighbours I had grown up with. I think I've only made one friend throughout junior high school and high school because they sat next to me in choir class and they actually talked to me.

I've never been to a real relationship before. The closest thing I've had was back when I was in 9th or 10th grade, I suppose a boy in my grade, Jace. He wasn't popular at all and was very silent. Jace took an interest in me and started to talk to me during the gym class that we shared together.

Eventually, I found out that he had hit on my friends in some way or another. I saw that he was actually interested in having a relationship with me. I didn't want to be mean so we eventually exchanged phone numbers and we started talking with each other.

Not long after, Jace began to show his true colors and wanted to date me. I didn't want to date him as it made me uncomfortable. My mum convinced me to give him a try, even though I said it made me uncomfortable. I said I wanted to know him better before I date him and get more serious about 'it'.

We texted and went to the cinema once. I tried to keep it a secret that we're talking and hanging out because I was embarrassed by the whole idea. Eventually, as time passed by, we hung out at a shop and he held my hand. I got very uncomfortable with it. Jace asked me if I was ok with it, and of course, I lied and said 'yes'. I don't know why, I just couldn't figure out why I couldn't just be honest and said 'no'.

After that, I stopped talking to him entirely because I was so embarrassed and uncomfortable by it all. I felt really bad that I didn't say anything to him at all. I still regret it all, but what's done is done.

My biggest problem is keeping all my troubles and problems to myself. I've only noticed signs of depression and anxiety in myself in the past year. Before, I didn't know much about either, but the more I looked, the more I noticed the symptoms of it being similar to my behavior.

It took me a long time to come to terms with it, to accept that I may have depression and anxiety. I spent a long time waiting for my sadness to go away, denying the fact that I may have mental illnesses, trying to deal with these things on my own.

I thought I helped everyone else, but I actually hurt those I really love. Before, I told everyone I could get really upset from holding my emotions and would sometimes lash it all out on my sister. Driving home by myself I'd sit and cry and I wouldn't know why I'm crying. When I had to walk home and pretend everything was going on just fine, it only hurt me more.

Even though I hadn't sought professional help and had my mental illness diagnosed professionally, it helped me that at least my mum and my sister knew about this and helped me with it. It felt like I was set free of something that tied me down.

I was so scared that they might think I'm overreacting or faking it or might think of me less because of it. I still haven't told any of my friends because I don't know how. I'm scared that they might think of me negatively afterwards. I know it may not be, but it seems like that in my eyes.

When I first told my mum, she offered to take me to a therapist, seeing as she didn't understand about these kinds of stuff. I was scared at that time and I said 'no'. Now, I've asked a couple of times to be checked out and to see a therapist, but so far, nothing has been done. My sister agrees that I should seek a therapist, but she doesn't have authority so it's just a mere suggestion.

Telling at least one person about it makes you feel like you've changed your world because it's not your little secret anymore and others have the ability to understand. They might just help you if they can/want to. That person can be anyone in your life, really. It could be someone in front of you whom you took for granted. Don't try to walk through it alone. Don't bottle it up.

Take As Much Time As You Need to Open Up: *Mick*

TW: *Mental Illness, Self-Harm, Substance Abuse, Suicidal Thought*

I'd say my depression really set at around 7th grade, everything was kind of going to hell around that time. My parents drank more than they usually do. I was moving to a new school. Recently, I was hurt by somebody I trusted. I'd usually sit on my bed, not wanting to alarm my parents. I'd grown irritated of their drinking; I didn't want to speak to them. I know I'd only make the situation worse.

One night, when everyone was asleep, I started cutting myself. It was such a relief, but my dad had found out. I stopped for a while, but once we moved to our new place, the feeling of being alone and of being helpless was still around.

My parents rarely drink now, which I am thankful for, but when they did, it was absolute torture. They drank due to stress. They'd only fight when they're intoxicated, and that irritated me the most. I tried to block it out so much but no matter what I did, it didn't help. That's why I relied on cutting. As stupid as it sounds, I thought cutting was a good way to relieve the stress I felt from their fights. I've told them I don't like it, I don't care anymore.

I realized that they're fantastic and loving parents, and that alcohol was their way to cope with stress. I mean, cutting used to be my way to cope with stress so I can't argue that what they're doing was unhealthy. Cutting is also unhealthy, I used to do it. Who am I to judge, anyway? I wasn't better than them in terms of what things to do in desperate times.

I'm still in school, just a freshman this year. I'm not as well known and I usually don't get mad at people, but I try my best to keep my friends happy. I hate to think that they'd be forced to endure some unbearable pain as I have, sort of. So if they are, I want to be able to ease it up, even if it's just a little. I have only a few friends whom I trust dearly.

I met the majority of them in my PE, Art, and Theatre class. For PE, I met about 3, yet I mainly talked to one. She's really open, emotional, and sad. I tried my best to make her laugh. For Art, I have a few who are really nice and welcoming and funny. Finally, for Theatre, they're boisterous and gleeful, so I'm glad that I don't have to worry about them committing suicide if depression gets to them.

I don't have a love life. It was also another factor to my depression, making me constantly think "no one could love me," and "I can't trust anyone with my heart if they can't love me," and so I always pushed others away when they claimed to care for me.

One night I remember threatening a friend I was going to jump off of the room. Thankfully she stopped me and told me I needed to talk to someone, so I promised her and did so.

I went to my science teacher, I trusted him the most out of all the adults that were currently in my life. When I opened up to him about everything that caused me to feel the way I did, he reached out for my hand and looked me dead in the eye. "This isn't your fault. None of it is. You're never alone in this."

After leaving that classroom, I felt as if a huge burden was lifted off of my chest. After speaking to him, I realized that opening up to someone does help. I've recently recovered, my arms are better and I am more than happy with my parents.

One thing I'd say to you is: don't think "Ah nobody cares, why should I even open up?" I know it's cliché, but someone is always willing to listen. Opening up is much easier to say than to do, trust me it took me a month after I made the promise to my friend to open up to my teacher. In the end, once you open up and get the proper help the weight on your soul will be lifted.

Keep fighting. Now that I've kept fighting I realize that there are people who do care and who will listen. Trust me, I realized that there are people who do care and who will listen, and to add to that take as much time as you need to open up. It's hard to do and hard to find the right friend to open up to, but once you do, it'll be worth it.

You Deserve a Happy Life: *Storm*

TW: Substance Abuse, Mental Illness, Abuse, Violence, Blood, Death

Dare I say, my home life wasn't very good at all. My home life seemed good from the outside, but it was bad on the inside. My father had just got us from my drug-addicted and strict mother; he was just getting sober from alcoholism. He was a war veteran with PTSD, so he had a lot of struggles. I was about 10 years old when I moved in with my father.

When I turned 13, everything went downhill. I already had a hard life when my mother had me for the first 10 years of my life. She had an abusive boyfriend that beat my sisters and me with belts and with his hands until we were covered with bruises. I took most of it because I was the oldest of 3 sisters. My sisters Rain and Summer were 3 and 5, and I was 8. My mother popped pills, partied, and got drunk. I had to take care of my sisters.

When I turned 13, my father met this horrible girl, Lisa. She was so manipulative that he fell for her. She ended up abusing him emotionally and physically, he never laid a hand on her. He started drinking and popping pills, he forgot about my sisters and me.

Lisa had 3 kids that were 11, 8, and 6. I took care of them too. I never had a childhood because of all this. Lisa hated my sisters and me because my father gave us more attention than she got from him. He made sure we got food and clothes even though Lisa made him go bankrupt. I went back to my 'sober' mother and my father finally kicked Lisa out.

My father was finally sober again for 2 weeks. When we came back, we spent only a week with him before he died. He died when he was 37 years old from being hit by 5 bullets out of 6 bullets that were shot by someone he thought he could trust. I almost lost my life too.

I ran to my father's aid and tried to wake him up. When I saw his blood on my hands, I panicked. I lifted his head up, got more blood on me. It got all over my clothes, my hands. His blood was all over me because I hugged him and cried, begging for him to come back. Rain was just 12 years old, Summer was just 10.

After that, my depression, anxiety disorder, and ADHD got worse, I developed PTSD and major depressive disorder along with the depression I already had. I was then sent to my mother. Everything was okay at first, and then she started popping pills.

I started drinking and smoking weed myself, I lost my virginity at 15. I fell down a hole because of the loss of my father, my mother never bothered to guide me in the right direction. I lived in poverty. After I turned 16, I was forced to work. I paid for groceries. I tried to make sure my sisters ate before me because I was the only one able to take care of them.

At the 8th of August 2018, I was taken away by child services to live in a foster home with my sisters. My grandparents got us out right away. Now I'm almost adopted and living a happier, healthier life with my grandparents.

I admit that it wasn't easy, trying to live a healthier life. There were times where I just dropped, or when PTSD just took over me, or desperate for weed and alcohol. I remembered my sisters, my life when we were kids, how alcohol and the misuse of drugs almost killed me and the people I love. I remember that they deserve to be happy, that I deserve to be happy. I deserve a life free of substance abuse.

Don't Let Negativity Influence Your Life: *Rose*

TW: Self-Harm, Suicide Attempt, Mental Illness, Violence

No, I didn't have depression or any problems with my anything (I think) but my best friend Eva did. I met Eva online. We played an online game together 5 years ago and I've seen her twice in my life, so we actually rarely met in real life. It feels like we knew each other for years, though. We told each other things all the time, I trusted her a lot and she trusted me a lot.

I knew that she had been cutting a lot for a while, probably since before September. She texted me once, saying, "I have a pair of scissors in my hand and I feel an urge to cut." I always tried to talk to her about other things that didn't have anything to do with self-harming to get her mind off it.

A few weeks ago she gave in and everything went horribly wrong. She had cut too deep and needed to go to the hospital. Eva had to get stitched up. They had been talking about getting her professional help but it didn't really help and she stopped. Last Friday she did it again. Same thing, she cut too deep and they called 911 to help her as they didn't know what to do.

Now she's been taken to a mental health hospital. It affects me as well. In the last few months, I had really bad stomach aches and the doctor never knew why I felt like that. They found no actual physical reasons behind it. After going to the hospital, I told my parents all about it. I have to admit, letting it out really helps me with my stomach pain and now my stomach hurts less.

Eva had problems with her father. They're both temperamental and stubborn. They kind of bumped into each other and my mother said it had to do with genes because Eva's mother wasn't mentally healthy too. I don't know anything about mental health things but I actually doubt it's hereditary. Luckily, I don't have problems with mine. My sister has problems with her mental health as well but a psychiatrist is enough to help her.

I was watching TV when I heard the news about her incident. I got a text saying her condition was fragile and that she was being brought to the hospital as soon as they possibly could. All my emotions came out, I started to cry and shaking terribly. To think about it, I'm kind of happy she cut too deep now because that means she's hospitalized and gets the help she desperately needs.

No, I don't have lovers, but my other friend Lila had problems concerning the boy she liked, Luke. He kept breaking her heart like wanting to be with her then he broke up with her, then he asked her to be his again, and so on like a never-ending cycle. That went on a while. They met each other at a birthday party. They started seeing each other more.

In the end, Lila had a sleepover with her friend Allison and Luke was having a fight with Allison at the same time. Lila and Luke weren't dating at that time, but Luke texted Lila saying he wanted to date her. Lila said no, and that Luke should make up with Allison before dating her. Luke was dismissive and being so rude about it. Lila was furious and she tore a jumper from him and burned it outside.

We are both still in school. I do have a moderately ok social life and pretty good interactions, but I can't say so for Eva. Actually, I don't know for Eva. Could be nice, could be not, but she mainly talks about her problems with her father.

I like it, to be honest. Having her talking to me means she's not handling this thing alone. Her getting hospitalized means she's getting the proper help she needs. I worry about her, but at least I know she's not alone in this. Any true friend would.

Any Problem Is a Real Problem:
Tenma

TW: Suicidal Thought, Mental Illness, Involuntary Coming Out, Bully

I don't actually know if it counts as suicidal, but I have thought about death for a while. I kind of crave it sometimes, but not all the time. Sometimes I do think about it, sometimes I don't. Often I think about like "if I die, will people care?" and on other occasions, I think about like "I don't want to die yet."

I don't know when exactly I started having these thoughts, probably in high school. I'm what you say a nihilist, and I think these thoughts first arrived because of my semi-depressive episodes. Back then, I didn't really know who to reach out. What to do.

It was a constant battle between the urge to give in and kill myself and the surviving instincts I have. Might be a little too extra on drawing the picture, but you get the idea, don't you?

If I must say, my home life is just ok. I make jokes about my broken family, I'm rather distant with my parents, I try to find the answers to my mental problems on my own. There are literally no ears for me to talk about this to. I hate the fact that my parents are so religious and would link my depression to religion. I hate that they are totally in the dark about this.

Actually, I didn't know they're divorced until the end of 2012. Even then, I couldn't care less. I always thought they divorced from a long time ago. The reason for it's because my father has moved out before, they're just legally severing the knot. None of them has remarried, and I don't have any siblings at all.

My social life is ok. Not the best, but not the worst either. I try to be a clown whenever I have to attend social gatherings. Saying dark jokes, self-deprecation jokes, they don't have a clue. The truth is, I hate my classmates. I can't really explain the hate.

I don't hate learning, and I know I'll get learning in school, but the inhabitants stress me out. I don't like going to school at all, where you have to put up a fake happy face and pretend you like these people around you.

I don't have enemies. I have friends, two kinds of friends, actually. One, I can just say 'hi' and no more and the other, I can genuinely trust and talk things to freely without judgment. Most of them fall under the prior category, not even 30% of them falls to the latter category. I met them at debating club or my old middle school friends.

Occasionally, I can talk to them about my deteriorating mental state. They're all quite supportive. Some don't really help me with my problems, but I appreciate the help some do give. I just immediately assume everyone hates me.

It's weird, to be honest. I easily assume people hate me but I'm pretty much sociable and I've no enemies. The thing is, no one really talks to me. I still pretty much hate myself, not going to lie.

My bisexuality might've contributed to the fact that I hate myself. I don't remember exactly when I started realizing my sexuality. Maybe I was around 13 – 14. Wait, no, 11, I think I was 11. I liked a guy once. I liked him from a distance and told a few people about it. Accidents happen and the news spread from ear to ear.

The ones that knew (not from me) sort of bullied me. Made fun of me, told my crush I liked him, you know all that. He sort of avoided me now. Thankfully, my parents never found out. I have no intention of letting them know. One teacher knew back then, some of my friends do too. Don't be like me. Consult about your problems as soon as it starts, so the healing process might be easier.

Know How to Deal With Your Problems: *Autumn*

TW: Mental Illness, Bully, Self-Harm, Suicidal Thought, Suicide Attempt, LGBT-Phobia

I think I've had depression since 6th grade. I mean, it all started in 6th grade. I was bullied before and I was scared I'd be bullied again. Turns out, I developed severe clinical depression and anxiety.

At 7th grade, it did get better, but it got worse later on. At 8th grade, I was really depressed. I quit softball, writing, pretty much everything I ever quite enjoyed. I didn't want to do anything at all. Like, ever. I just wanted to go to bed and cry my eyes out.

Over the summer, it had gotten so bad. It's much worse than before and I had started cutting myself. I took my brother's knife and cut myself. At first, it wasn't much. I thought it'd be a one thing kind of thing, but it wasn't. I isolated myself from everyone.

I honestly thought I'd get better in high school. I didn't. I felt empty. I felt empty all the time and I'm supposed to feel happy. I mean, I have ok grades, a boyfriend, I shouldn't feel this numb. To get rid of it, I cut again, and again, and again.

In September, I had a mental breakdown. I was screaming and crying yet I was alone. I felt like I was alone. I didn't like this feeling, so I did what most would do in my situation, I'm sure of it. I cut myself again. At first, they were on my arms and legs, but then I thought, nothing was off-limits. There were no limitations on my cutting, so why should I stop?

I looked up to the mirror and I held a knife up to my neck. I thought no one would ever care and I was going to do it. I somehow couldn't. I don't know what stopped me, but I just couldn't force myself to do it. So I put the knife down and went to bed. I wanted to die but I just couldn't force myself to do it, something I am now glad I'd not done.

Something happened and at the beginning of October, my mum found out I was cutting. It happened so fast. I was so frightened; I didn't know what they'd think about it. My mum just held me tight and cried. My dad searched my room and took out all my knives.

They took me to a mental hospital. The hospital said that I needed to come there after school every day for a month until 6 PM. I did all that. I didn't gain anything from that; it was just to make sure that I didn't hurt myself again.

Whilst I was there, I dealt with my first breakup. He started to realize that I wasn't straight and all that scared him. I felt like my friends didn't care about me. My grades plummeted. I had bad grades and my parents grounded me from doing anything. I was alone with myself and I became suicidal. I just didn't want to deal with the pain anymore.

Something happened and I started seeing a therapist and a psychiatrist. My therapist was an amazing woman. Being able to talk to someone about how I'm feeling without that someone judging me and even help me with my problems is just terrific. My psychiatrist prescribed me some medication and though I wasn't the happiest, at least I wasn't suicidal.

Over the summer I had my ups and downs and near the end of it, it became worse. I was at a beach. I ran into the bathroom and I started crying. I was told to be happy but I didn't know how to be happy. I wanted to but I couldn't. Looking back at it I know that I couldn't have done anything and that I should've tried to explain it better to my parents, but I didn't.

Now at the beginning of this year, I was really scared and alone. I didn't have many friends. With the help of my therapist and the few good friends I'd gotten then, I started to make more friends that could support me. I also have grown to love art and use it as a good coping mechanism. I cut out some toxic people from my life and started to focus on the good parts of life as best as I could. I'm still depressed. I still have anxiety.

It gets better over time. I acknowledge the fact that I still have a long way to go to be really happy, but little steps matter. I'm still depressed but I'm learning how to deal with it instead of shoving it under the rug. It helped the people around me and myself. I don't know how long I will live, but I will try my best to be happy. I know I'm not going to be successful anytime soon. I know I hurt others, but I know how to deal with it.

To those who are struggling, I want you to know that it will get better, that there is something to look forward to. I promise you. You may not know when but know that things will get better. I myself didn't know when but I kept my head up. Try to get help. I promise you that it will help a lot. Don't bottle it all up to yourself.

Live Your Own Life: *Jaidlynn*

TW: Abuse, Sexual Abuse, Suicidal Thought, Bully

How do I start? It started when I was 3, I think. My biological father was physically and mentally abusive towards my mother and me. My mother tried to escape from his clutches but unfortunately, she failed. I was sexually abused many times by him until I was 5. It was horrible, to sum it up. We managed to run from him and he was arrested. My mum, my brother, and I lived together for a year, perhaps.

We moved to my mother's boyfriend's house. Unfortunately, I went through another assault by my babysitter's son. Eventually, my mother and her boyfriend got married to each other. At that time, both my brother and I had considered him as our real father. I was desperate for another as my biological one was abusive.

My brother and I were homeschooled so we didn't have friends and none of my family really liked my stepfather. Time made us move on. I had surgeries for a disease called articular vascular malformation.

Four-and-a-half years later, we moved to Florida, away from our relatives. By then, my brother and I started to notice the little changes in our stepfather's behavior. He started restricting the little freedom we had, dividing all the chores we all should've done together to the 2 of us only, slowly treating us like servants instead of his children.

Two years ago I finally met my best friend. By then, we almost never had free time. Most of it was used by chores and schoolwork.

As time went on, the abuse started to go verbal. By then I almost never slept. I was constantly stressed by schoolwork, chores, and trying my best to protect my brother, as he seemed to be his main meal in abusing. My brother and I learnt to wear 'masks', to show no emotions whatsoever.

Finally, 6 months ago my brother and I learnt that we would be going up to visit our relatives in the north. We were so happy. Three months went by as we lived far high up in the north, alternating between family members.

Escalating to about 3 weeks before we had to go back down, they discovered our 'secret'. I genuinely thought we'd stay up there instead of going to that hellhole, but because of the law stuff, we had to go back down.

The next day, my stepfather had made us breakfast. Oh right, I've forgotten to mention. Usually, our previous meals down in Florida consist of fruits for breakfast and a sandwich for lunch, but the sandwiches were usually held to the barest minimum, it was mostly bread. So we were literally skin and bones.

Anyway, he made us breakfast because he needed us to organize the camper; basically, it was just to energize us to work harder for him. Fortunately for us, the child services then came and took us out of that house.

We lived with my mum in a shelter they provided us. She, amazingly, was oblivious to all the abuse that happened. Unfortunately, due to the fact that we literally lost everything, she sent us back up to our relatives, where we have been living together ever since.

I think the worst part of the abuse was the fact that I'd gotten so used to it that I barely had any emotions left. Since I had wore a 'mask' for so long... it physically saved me, not going to lie, but I'm pretty sure I've lost the very thing that made me human in the first place.

At some point before we were sent up to the north, we almost killed ourselves. We were utterly depressed. We had been hit, abused, told we're useless, betrayed by our family. I actually died during one of my surgeries, yet no one noticed. Yes, not even my brother did. We wore our 'masks' often, me more so than my brother, which was the reason why he's more prone to emotions than I am. No, that's not an achievement.

I've said before that I was homeschooled, and I still am. I decided to continue it because I want to graduate early and get all that over with. Sometimes I got bullied by the kids from my neighborhood, but I usually ignored them. Most of them, if not all, actually tend to avoid me.

Even now, I visit a youth group and become more active, yet I'm still avoided. I asked one of my acquaintances, "Why am I avoided?" Assuming she knew the answer. She did, actually. She told me that it's because according to them, I was cold. They avoid me because I don't show a lot of emotions, leaving me with a blank look. Add to the fact that I'm asexual, they see me as this emotionless weirdo.

I would want you to know that you will make mistakes. That's for sure, but make sure that you recover from those mistakes. Don't hide in fear, don't hide in the shadows. Live your life. Your life is yours, not someone else's. If you need help, don't stop until you get that help you need. If you want something, fight with all your might to get it. Don't hide away like me.

Final Message

Many kids are born to parents who aren't ready
to have them
Many people who aren't ready to have kids are
forced to have them
Many kids are so insecure that they had to make
others insecure
Many kids are triggered by the thought of going
to school/their house
Many kids felt more at ease on the internet than
in their house
Many kids resented their parents and wish they
weren't born
Is that supposed to be normal?